Lamington National Park

NATIONAL PARKS OF
QUEENSLAND

NATIONAL PARKS OF QUEENSLAND

READER'S DIGEST

The editors wish to thank the officers of the
Queensland National Parks and Wildlife Service for their advice
and assistance; in particular, Don Marshall.

Some of the material in this book first appeared in
Reader's Digest Wild Australia, first published in 1984;
republished in 1998.

**WILD AUSTRALIA was edited and designed by
Reader's Digest (Australia) Pty Limited**
All travelling photographic commissions were
undertaken by Robin Morrison

Project Editor   Art Editor
David Underhill   Anita Sattler

Editor • Robert Campbell
Assistant Editor • Françoise Toman
Research Editor • Vere Dodds

READER'S DIGEST NATIONAL PARKS OF QUEENSLAND
was edited and designed by Reader's Digest (Australia) Pty Limited

Project Editor   **Art Editor**
Shirley Macnab   Anita Sattler

FIRST EDITION 1987, SECOND EDITION 1998
Published by Reader's Digest (Australia) Pty Limited
26 - 32 Waterloo Street, Surry Hills, NSW 2010.

National Library of Australia Cataloguing-in-Publication data:
National parks of Queensland.

Includes index.
ISBN 0 86449 333 9.

1. National parks and reserves – Queensland –
Guide-books. 2. Queensland – Description and travel
– 1976- – Guide-books. I. Reader's Digest Services.

919.43'04

CONTENTS

INTRODUCTION

What's in a name?

AUSTRALIA HAS more than 500 so-called national parks. Their status was proclaimed by state and territorial authorities under policies that used to differ widely. Many parks, especially among the 300-odd declared in Queensland, are mere islets or scraps of bush as small as one hectare. Some are huge, but so remote and inhospitable that their existence has little public relevance. And in a few parks, visitors have no place at all – the sites are really animal sanctuaries, or strictly for research.

Nature reserves of that sort are important. But people expect direct benefits from something called a national park. The term should denote a significant area capable of accommodating the right of substantial numbers of visitors to enjoy its natural features and learn from them. Too many 'parks' do not meet this prescription. Bestowed indiscriminately, a proud title loses meaning. The effect, though surely not intended, is sometimes to mislead and disappoint the public.

In offering a frank comparison of park attractions, we aim not to dictate readers' tastes but to provide them with a fair basis for making choices of their own. This guide presents a revision of information first amassed in the Reader's Digest book *Wild Australia*. That remains the only single publication to appraise such a large number of the country's national parks.

Simply identifying all of them for the first edition demanded a trailblazing effort. Because of the pace of acquisition and change since the 1950s, no complete list had existed. Even the names of some parks were difficult to establish. Legally gazetted titles conflicted with common usage, or hard-pressed administrators saved paperwork by lumping smaller sites anonymously into groups.

Financial strictures beset all parks services. Areas may be designated by the stroke of a pen, but funds for public facilities are a long time coming. Often as our researchers sought to define the merits of a park, they were told: 'We'd really rather you didn't mention that one'. A state information officer, confessing his ignorance of a newly acquired property, explained: 'We sent a fellow out there once to get material for a brochure. But he couldn't find the place...'

Not without qualms, a system of rating was instituted. Judgments behind all the ticks and crosses in the reference sections were made in consultation with park authorities, but they remain subjective and debatable. So are our assumptions of the broad areas of visitor interest. 'Scenic enjoyment' in one park derives from the intimate charm of a single waterfall; in another it may come from the sweeping grandeur of a whole mountain range or coastline. 'Day activities' indicates a good choice of things to do – but who can predict preferences? 'Family camping' supposes a desire to stay put for perhaps a week, in conditions not unduly primitive. 'Hard bushwalking' in most cases points to the challenge of backpack trekking and overnight camping.

Pictorially we have aimed for realism, not idealism. Rather than gathering in a selection of the prettiest and luckiest shots ever taken in national parks, we offer the results of one man's efforts. Robin Morrison, the touring photographer, was advised and guided by rangers in some parks. But for the most part he took his chances like any other member of the travelling public, limited in time and at the mercy of the weather.

After his year-long assignment for *Wild Australia*, covering more than 200 locations from Tasmania to North West Cape, Morrison had a suggestion. 'Tell your readers,' he said, 'that anything I did, they can do. With any luck they may see even more. And you can also tell them that most of the finest scenery in this country is not all that far away or hard to get to.'

He was right. In spite of the obvious modification of desirable countryside by two centuries of European settlement, unspoilt landscapes lie remarkably close to most major centres of population. Australians, nearly 90 per cent of whom lead their everyday lives in urban or suburban environments, need not go far to refresh themselves and recover their sense of community with more natural surroundings.

This book is published in the hope that readers will reach a fuller understanding of what remains of our physical heritage, that they will care for it, and above all that they will enjoy it.

THE EDITORS

Tully Gorge National Park

PART ONE
The nature of Australia

Nothing in nature happens without a reason. Powerful influences shaped Australia's landscapes. Now they dictate where its unique plants grow. Knowing the meaning that lies behind scenery makes it all the more enjoyable.

Ancient but scarcely trodden, the Bungle Bungle Ranges stand in lonely dignity east of the Kimberleys, WA

How the stage was set

WEATHERING, given time enough, levels any land surface. Heights are worn down and basins are filled with the debris, to be compressed into fresh rock. With the ups and downs removed and gravity equalised, rock erosion stops. Only overlying soils or sands are subject to further attack.

But awesome pressures work tirelessly on the earth's crust. Sometimes they warp it, tilting an old land mass to a new angle of elevation. Sometimes the crust buckles, and another generation of mountains is thrust up. Molten

Eroded rock layers at Kings Canyon, NT, are tilted almost vertically. Once they formed towering domes

material from below blasts or oozes through weak points in the crust. The height of the land is varied and erosion resumes. All these events have occurred time and again in Australia.

Rocks of the Australian land mass differ astonishingly in their age, their composition and their capacity to resist erosion. They include the world's oldest known formations as well as some of the youngest, and everything from the softest clays to the most impermeable granites. Climatic conditions vary widely. So do the surrounding oceans in their behaviour – some destroy the land, some help it to build. Most diverse of all are the soils produced by rock erosion, and the plant life they can sustain.

Flat landscapes, virtually featureless and usually parched, prevail across more than half of the continent. Weathering is all but complete, for much of this land has been undisturbed for eons. Ranges thrust up in the west, made from rocks that formed more than 3000 million years ago, are reduced to a smoothed shield, rarely outcropping from its sandy cover. Once-mighty rivers that drained the heights – and helped demolish them – can be traced only in chains of dismal salt pans. Seabeds to the east have become plains, at best marginally fertile.

Remnants of mountain systems in Central Australia and the far north and northwest are younger, though the age of their rocks still staggers the mind. Ranges such as the Musgraves and the Hamersleys, along with many in the Kimberleys and Arnhem Land, originated more than 1000 million years ago. Pushed up, they towered higher than Mt Kosciusko is now. All are in the late stages of destruction – but nature has not wasted them.

By the time the MacDonnell Ranges were forced up in Central Australia, perhaps 200-300 million years ago, material eroded from the Musgraves had re-formed as a bed of sedimentary rock. South of the MacDonnells, it was distorted and broken by their upheaval. Immense chunks of sandstone or cemented boulders were elevated at all angles, to be swamped later by a returning sea. New depos-

its of sediments buried all but the highest summits. Now, severely worn in their turn, the broad domes we call Ayers Rock and the Olgas jut incongruously from the central plain.

Nearby Mt Conner, similarly created, presents a surprising contrast. It is table-topped, and noticeably eroded only at the sides. When this mass was pushed up, its layers of sediments chanced to remain horizontal under their original capping of toughened material. To the north, on apparently similar country, are piled the huge boulders called the Devil's Marbles. Here a cracked block of granite has been eroded across and down all its joints. Such variations are essentially the products of chance – what types of rocks are exposed, and how their former bedding planes are tilted.

Ocean levels rose and fell – or the land fell and rose – repeatedly. Invading seas often divided ancestral Australia into islands. New rock material included increasing quantities of calcium from the remains of marine animals. Pavings of porous limestone formed widely. High and dry now, many are noted for their subterranean cave systems, eaten out by percolating rainwater.

Sometimes the seas were remarkably warm. Corals built reefs in the Gordon River district of Tasmania 350-400 million years ago. But 100 million years later an icecap reached to the Kimberleys, and Tasmania lay beside the South Pole. And after a further 100 million years, according to plant fossil evidence, Australia and Antarctica shared a subtropical climate. Like all continental land masses, they have been on the move.

At first all the continents were probably contained in a single cluster, which seems to have broken in two well over 200 million years ago. After that Australia, Antarctica, New Guinea, India, Africa, Arabia and South America were joined in a southern supercontinent which scientists call Gondwanaland. But the earth's rigid crust was fracturing. Rifts opened, and new molten matter welled up to force the modern continents apart.

Widening oceans filled the gaps. The crust

TRACING A VANISHED LANDSCAPE

ROCKS are of three types. Sedimentary rocks form from the debris of older rocks and the remains of aquatic animals. Sandstones, limestones and shales are commonest. Igneous rocks form from molten material. If it cools without reaching the air, it usually turns into granite. Lava cooling on the surface makes a basalt. Metamorphic rocks are the result of pressure and heat on sedimentary or igneous rocks. Sandstone becomes quartzite, shale becomes slate, granite becomes gneiss.

Sedimentary rocks form in flat layers, varying in hardness. Squeezed by earth movements, they bend into folds. Erosion removes the softer material in a fold, and only the stubs of tough ridges remain

Molten material pushing up into a fold forms granite. Erosion leaves a tough core (left). But if the material builds a volcano, the last of it may set as a hard-wearing plug of trachyte or rhyolite (right)

Beds of metamorphic rock are too rigid to fold. Instead they crack into blocks that are tilted and pushed up. Rates of erosion depend on the angle of tilt, as well as on the composition of the blocks

itself separated into mobile plates. Fifteen major plates and a few small ones now restlessly cover the globe. The section Australia rides on – along with India, New Guinea and part of New Zealand – is rafting very slowly north-westward because its eastern and southern neighbours are expanding.

Violent earth movements are inevitable at the edges of a plate. But Australia lies far from any collision zone. Since its isolation it has been the least disturbed of the continents. The last truly catastrophic event – the production of eastern and central Tasmania's dolerite columns and cappings by the intrusion of molten matter into old sandstones – was about 165 million years ago. Many geologists associate it with the start of the Gondwanaland breakup.

Early mountain ranges on the eastern mainland were well worn down by then. Soon all that remained of them were cores of tough granite, solidified from molten material that had flowed up into their folds. Often it is this granite that forms the summits of mountains that have been thrust up more recently.

Parts of the Eastern Highlands – notably the Snowy Mountains and Victorian Alps – were pushed up about 65 million years ago. A second phase of general uplift in the east, remarkably gentle, took place within the past 3-7 million years. A probable cause was the slumping of the crust far inland, under the weight of sediments from one ocean or sea after another. The slumped parts, since covered by more recent porous rock, underlie the reservoirs of underground water known collectively as the Great Artesian Basin.

To compensate for this sinking of the crust, land near the east coast gradually rose. It formed tablelands with a barely perceptible slope. Warping to create mountain ranges occurred only in the last stages of uplift, and at the seaward extremity. Similar forces working in the west had a more drastic effect. There the ancient rock shield was pinned down by coastal sediments. It snapped at the point where it emerged, and now its uptilted edge forms a rampart nearly 1000 km long backing the coastal plain on which Perth is centred. The Darling Range is misnamed – it should be the Darling Scarp. But in its influence on climate and vegetation, it acts in much the same way as a mountain system would.

Near-coastal ranges and the coastlines themselves have the freshest and most changeable landforms. All the forces of erosion are seen actively at work. Volcanic activity can be traced. So can the variation of soil fertilities, and the rivalries of plant communities under different climatic regimes. Everywhere, the lie of the land and the look of the landscape are intimately related.

THE OLDEST THING ON EARTH

Electric probing mars a history-making zircon – enlarged 200 times

OUR PLANET was born 4500-4600 million years ago, astronomers believe. It took an unknown time to cool enough to form a solid crust. The most ancient rocks found, in Western Australia and Greenland, are about 3800 million years old. But they are sedimentary – made of something even older.

'A clue emerged in 1983 at Mt Narryer, 200 km inland from Carnarvon, WA. Microscopic grains of zircon were discovered in quartzite rocks.

Using a new electrical probing technique, scientists measured the proportions of uranium and lead contained as impurities in the zircons.

Uranium loses its radioactivity and turns into lead at a known rate. So the age of the zircons could be calculated. Four of the tiny stones, it seems, must have been formed between 4100 and 4200 million years ago. Until humans venture outside this solar system, they may never handle anything older.

Sun and rain: the great dictators

JUST AS ancient weathering shaped the land, present climates decide its clothing. Sunlight, temperature and moisture determine which trees or shrubs or grasses flourish where. And they govern the likelihood of wildfire – the other factor that sets apart the great plant families of Australia and rules over the appearance of natural landscapes.

Twisting statistics, Australians could boast the world's most generous share of rain. More of it falls, per person, than in any other country. But that is merely a reflection of the sparseness of population. In fact most of the continent is poorly watered and subject to high rates of evaporation. Over a vast sweep between southwestern Queensland and North West Cape, hot sunshine beats down for more than 3500 hours a year.

Mainland Australia straddles the southern hemisphere's belt of greatest air pressure. 'Highs' – cells of descending air as much as 4000 km wide, calm or rotating gently under clear skies – pass from west to east in an almost continuous chain. Troughs separating them, usually at intervals of four or five days, may bring cool changes but seldom much rain. North of the pressurised belt southeasterly breezes – the Trade Winds of sailing ship days – blow steadily from the Pacific. To the south of the belt the air flow is from the west, and much stronger.

The high-pressure belt changes its position seasonally. In winter it is centred over the middle of the continent. Tropical regions, except on the east coast, are parched. The southeasterlies, having deposited their ocean moisture on the coastal ranges, flow on unimpeded and arrive in the northwest dry, hot and dusty.

Southern Australia in winter is swept by a cold westerly air stream. Often this is whipped into chilling southwesterly gales because 'lows' – tight, churning cells of rising and condensing air – intrude from the Southern Ocean.

Rain is plentiful, except round the Bight, and the southeastern highlands get snow. But in much of New South Wales and subtropical Queensland, where the westerlies have dried out or do not reach, winter may be sunny.

In summer the belt of high pressure lies over Bass Strait. Rainfall is generally low in southern regions, though clear spells may be broken by squally changes. On most parts of the east coast down to Sydney, however, Pacific moisture is turned into liberal summer rains because the Trade Winds have also moved south.

From November to April, the far north has its 'Wet'. A zone of low pressure, originating over the Equator but shifting in summer to about the latitude of Darwin, sucks in a monsoon of saturated air from the northwest. Thundery showers drench the Kimberleys, the Top End and Cape York Peninsula day after day. In some seasons, but never predictably, the lows pass far enough south to bring flooding rains to Central Australia and outback regions of the southern and eastern states.

Summer is also the season of violent tropical cyclones. Only five or six a year affect the coast, and their destructive power wanes as soon as they pass inland. But the spiralling cloud mass of a decaying cyclone brings heavy rain over an ever-widening area, perhaps for a week or more. Semi-arid regions, particularly in the northwest, receive much of their moisture in this erratic way.

Regardless of average patterns, year-by-year rainfall over most of Australia is notoriously variable. Port Hedland, WA, for example, is listed as having a median annual fall of just over 300 mm. But that figure is merely the product of actual readings as low as 30 mm a year and as high as 1000 mm or more. Apart from the monsoon zone, rainfall is consistently good only in Tasmania, on most of the Victorian, New South Wales and Queensland coasts, and in winter in the extreme southwest of

Western Australia. It is no coincidence that all these regions have mountains close to the sea.

Air flowing off sunlit oceans is always loaded with evaporated moisture. But to condense into clouds that precipitate rain, it must be cooled. The usual cause of cooling is elevation: air temperatures drop by about 5°C with each 1000 metres of altitude. A fall in pressure when air flows into a 'low', or a collision of different air masses, can cause the necessary uplift and trigger a storm. However, no one can say exactly where that will happen. Truly reliable rains occur only where moist air flows are blocked and forced upward by steep land.

Australia is not only the flattest of all continents, but also the lowest-lying. Counting mountain ranges, its average elevation is still a mere 300 metres above sea level. That makes it generally warmer than any other land mass in comparable latitudes. Far from being cooled, moist air flowing into many regions is heated up. The longer its journey, the hotter it gets – hence the heat waves that occasionally sear southern cities, including Hobart.

Summer northwesterlies, entering over the Great Sandy Desert between Port Hedland and Broome, have the longest possible low, flat run. If not diverted by atmospheric disturbances they can reach all the way to western NSW – 2500 km. Shade temperatures above 50°C are recorded there, in an arc from Bourke to Wilcannia and White Cliffs, more often than in any other district in Australia.

Superheated air flows hasten the evaporation of soil moisture and the desiccation of plants. In regions perennially short of rain – though with fertile soil – plant life has had to adapt in unusual ways. And where rains in most years are good enough to foster profuse growth, but they occasionally fail, the chance of devastation by fire is abnormally high. Again plants have found ways to cope – and even to benefit.

At the opposite end of the climatic scale, wide tracts of high country in the southeast and Tasmania lie under snow for months each year. Elsewhere, over a surprising area, plants contend with frost in winter and spring. In the south it results from inflows of chilled air after depressions. But frosts also occur well to the north, in places better known for their heat. In the high-pressure belt dominating mid-Australia in winter, cloud cover is rare and ground warmth starts passing into the upper atmosphere as soon as the sun goes down. Alice Springs has more frosty nights than any of the southern capitals except Canberra. On the east coast, the effects of elevation take frosts even farther north. Cooled air, sinking into valleys draining the Great Dividing Range, can ice the ground within 20 km of Cairns.

Parched, sunburnt sandplains reach into NSW at Mungo National Park – once part of a major waterway

Below: Air cooling over Kosicuszko National Park, NSW, sinks into the upper Murray Valley, forming a river of cloud

Right: Highland frost and vigorous tree growth join forces to crack capping rock in Girraween National Park, Qld

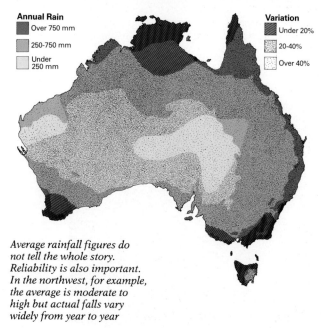

Annual Rain
- Over 750 mm
- 250-750 mm
- Under 250 mm

Variation
- Under 20%
- 20-40%
- Over 40%

Average rainfall figures do not tell the whole story. Reliability is also important. In the northwest, for example, the average is moderate to high but actual falls vary widely from year to year

13

Grandeur in the high country

MOUNTAINS are nature's showcases. Bared, they display every type and formation of rock. Erosion can be seen in action, with the effects of rain, wind, frost and chemical change accentuated by the force of gravity. And on vegetated slopes, the temperature gradients created by altitude give plant and animal life their fullest opportunity for variety.

Australia lacks the soaring peaks of the other continents and even of its island neighbours, New Guinea and New Zealand. In compensation, its high country is more accessible and less subject to dangerously sudden switches of weather. Its coastal uplands, especially in Queensland, offer a range of plant communities as wide as any in the world.

Scenically and economically, the Eastern Highlands chain is Australia's most significant mountain system. It curves from Cape York into western Victoria, more or less parallel to the coast, and resumes in Tasmania. Islands in Bass and Torres Straits, along with some off Queensland, are peaks emerging from drowned sections of the same system.

For most of their mainland length the highlands are the more elevated seaward side of a wide belt of tablelands. The Great Divide – where rivers start to flow inland, not to the Pacific Ocean – often occurs at lower altitudes well to the west. That shows how slowly the highlands rose in their final uplift, which was completed about 3 million years ago. Ancient rivers, already flowing east, had time to cut deeper courses as the land tipped up.

Movement was so gentle that buckling to produce ranges of fold mountains was limited to the eastern edge of the belt. Massive tilting of fractured blocks, to raise processions of peaks like the Southern Alps of New Zealand, was virtually non-existent. A spectacular exception is the Bellenden Ker Range, just south of Cairns, Qld. Even the summits of the Snowy Mountains and Victorian Alps are smooth granite tablelands. The Blue Mountains, west of Sydney, were just as flat. Layers of sandstone and shale were pushed up thousands of metres without shifting from their horizontal plane. Today's dramatic pillars, cliffs and ravines are simply the result of weathering – and it is far from finished.

Remnants of huge volcanic systems abound, especially about the Qld/NSW border and to the southwest in the Nandewar and Warrumbungle Ranges. These date from 15-25 million years ago. The later phase of eastern uplift brought new activity, but no big volcanoes were built. Most eruptions were easy upwellings of lava from fissures in the earth's crust.

Left: Glaciers sculpted the jagged peaks and walled lakes of southwest Tasmania

Most of the Great Dividing Range is a tableland cut by rivers – in this case the Shoalhaven River in Morton National Park, NSW

Worn quartzite domes in the Gammon Ranges, SA

layers, have contracted into clusters of tough hexagonal columns – Melbourne's Organ Pipes, for example.

But many basalts decompose quickly when exposed to air and water. They break down into fine, dark soils containing an unusual abundance of mineral nutrients for plants. It is the prevalence of basaltic – often called volcanic – soils, allied with high rainfall, that allows the Eastern Highlands their luxuriant growth of forests.

Tasmania's heights reveal a much older geological background. The region's main upheaval came 165 million years ago. Enormous tongues of molten material penetrated its original sandstone strata. They cooled as dolerite, which has a columnar 'organ pipe' structure similar to some basalts. Now, with almost all of the sandstone worn away, deep sheets of dolerite cover most of eastern and central Tasmania. Sheer-faced crags jut from a tableland so toughly capped that no rivers of significance have managed to cut courses. Instead this is a landscape sculpted by ice. Only in Tasmania can the full effects of glaciation during the last ice age, between 40 000 and 10 000 years ago, be seen. Mountains are chewed away at their sides. Moraines of rock debris trap deep alpine lakes. Countless little tarns, gouged by boulders dragged in a creeping cap of ice, glitter on the plateau.

West of the tableland, Tasmania's ranges have no intrusion of dolerite. They are of softer quartzite, now deeply dissected by gorges. High volumes of water, precipitated almost year-round in rain and snow, seize their chance to find steep courses to the sea between thickly forested slopes. Here are born the island's fast-flowing 'wild rivers', so enticing and precious to white-water adventurers.

No other mountains in Australia stand as tall as the Eastern Highlands, or have soils and rainfall to sustain comparable forest growth. Elsewhere the greatest fascination of higher

Hard basalt from ancient lava flows caps Mt Wilson, 950 metres up in Blue Mountains National Park, NSW

Lava flows continued, in fewer and fewer places, almost to the present day. The last coatings on the western plains of Victoria, where more than 20 000 square kilometres are covered, were laid less than 6000 years ago. Even more of the northern Queensland tablelands was blanketed not long before.

Old volcanoes are often marked now by cylinders of rock jutting into the sky. These are plugs made of the last molten material, solidified before it reached the air. It forms exceptionally hard rock – usually trachyte or rhyolite – that resists erosion while the surrounding cone is worn away.

Molten material that flows out as lava, however, turns into a basalt. Its hardness will vary according to its mineral content. Some basalts, reddish or chocolate brown and rich in iron, remain as protective cappings on tablelands or form thin bands sandwiched in the joints of older rocks. Others, cooling evenly in deep

country usually lies in its stark antiquity. The huge island-mountains of Uluru National Park, for example, or the eroded forms of the Flinders Ranges in South Australia, are individually more haunting than any eastern scene.

Major ranges in Central Australia and the northwest, such as the MacDonnells, the Hamersleys and those in the Kimberleys, are so aged and weathered that their heights lend them little distinction. Instead it is their depths, in the gorges cut by eons-old rivers, which provide the most memorable scenes – and the clearest insights into the structure of the continent.

THIS WAS THE HOTTEST SPOT OF ALL

MOUNT WARNING (left) is the 22-million-year-old central plug of Australia's biggest volcano. Remnants of its rim, straddling the Qld/NSW border across a diameter of about 40 km, survive in the McPherson, Tweed and Nightcap Ranges. All have steep scarps of tough basalt facing in towards Mt Warning, and gently sloping outer flanks.

Scientists can only guess at the original dimensions of the Tweed volcano, but it almost certainly stood taller than Mt Kosciusko is now. Rainforests ringing the rim, largely preserved in a chain of national parks, flourish on rich soils derived from the volcano's outpourings of lava. It is thought to have been active for about 3 million years.

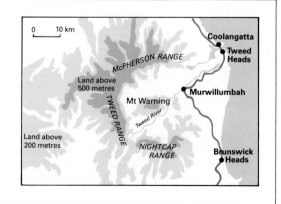

Fresh water: a precious bounty

RIVERS AND LAKES are scarce in Australia. Truly natural ones are even more rare. The Aborigines accepted that most water supplies were sporadic: the movements of the animals they hunted, and their own nomadic lives, were ruled by that fact. But European settlers chose accessible rivers and stayed put. They demanded that the water come to them – tamed.

Dams, weirs and levees were built to eliminate the extremes of drought and flood. Banks were straightened and obstacles removed to aid navigation. Flows were diverted to water livestock and irrigate crops. Supplies were drawn off not just for drinking and washing but also for industrial processes, and lately to fill hundreds of thousands of swimming pools.

Even in remote high country, a century or more ago, streams were altered by erosion of their headwater catchments. Forest logging was to blame. More recently, hydro-electric engineering has regulated many rivers, and created new lakes or raised old ones.

Queensland's Barron Falls, once the year-round tourist highlight of the Atherton Tablelands, now flow only in the wet season when the Tinaroo Dam overspills. The Snowy River is deprived of more than 2 million million litres a year by tunnelled diversion to the Murrumbidgee and Murray. The Murray itself is depleted, and salted by the leaching of minerals from cleared land. The Darling, contributing most of the Murray's water, can no longer fluctuate between a chain of billabongs and a flooding sheet hundreds of kilometres wide. Barrages and storage lakes hold it in check.

Where highland rainforests remain untouched, some unspoilt rivers are still to be found flowing in all seasons. Western Tasmania's are the most celebrated – but also the hardest to reach. Many national parks on the Great Dividing Range, however, give access to streams that spill from scarps in waterfalls or cascades, then plunge into ferny ravines.

More indicative of the real nature of most Australian waterways are the braided beds and floodplains of the Channel Country in western Queensland. They are nearly always dry. Even major rivers such as the Diamantina and Cooper Creek are ephemeral, flowing only after prolonged heavy rain. And it takes weeks of the most phenomenal flooding of the Channel Country before the vast salt pans of Lake Eyre are likely to fill.

Monsoon floodplains in the far north are scenes of remarkable annual transformation in plant and animal life. But when it happens, most such districts are inaccessible. The best a traveller can do to appreciate the contrast at Kakadu National Park, for example, is find time for two visits – one just before the wet season, and one as soon as possible after.

Most other national parks in the Northern Territory, and all the popular ones to the west from the Kimberleys to Kalbarri, are based on ancient, deeply cut gorges. Their rivers fluctuate seasonally, and in Central Australia most are ephemeral. The attraction for visitors, especially late in the dry season, may be not so much in the watercourses as in the grandeur of their walls. Often the gorges hold pockets of primitive, moist-climate palms and vines – relics of an age long past.

Rivers in the southwest are generally short-flowing and much changed by forest clearance and settlement. Inland, former drainage systems are marked by salt pans, arranged in a horseshoe pattern spanning 500 km. Similar forms extend from north of Lake Eyre to the Flinders Ranges and Eyre Peninsula, SA.

In western NSW, a more recently dried waterway is represented in the Willandra Lakes chain. Mungo National Park's stark lunette walls, like the rims of a moon crater, are built of sands blown from the bed of a lake that held ample water until about 20 000 years ago.

Water storage is so precious now that most natural lakes have been amplified by damming. Australia's deepest, Lake St Clair in Tasmania, was raised to serve power stations on the River Derwent. The greatest of all in area, Lake Argyle in the Kimberleys, was made by damming the Ord River.

Old estuaries, barred by sand ridges, form sizeable coastal lakes in NSW and eastern Victoria. But the streams feeding them are often interfered with, and the lakes themselves modified by settlement or heavy recreational use. Of the few that have been largely spared, outstanding examples are found in The Lakes National Park, Vic, and Myall Lakes National Park, NSW.

The Wimmera River, flowing by Little Desert National Park, gives trees a rare chance in western Victoria

THE HIDDEN RESERVOIRS

ARTESIAN water fell as rain – long ago and very far away. It lies under western Queensland and northwestern NSW, and reaches beneath the Central and South Australian deserts. But all of it came from the Eastern Highlands.

The Great Artesian Basin – really a group of basins separated by underground ridges – is a part of Australia that slumped millions of years ago under the weight of inland seas and their deposits. The sediments formed porous rock, to be capped later by impermeable shales. To balance the slumping, land at the eastern rim rose. Wherever the raised edge of the porous layer has been exposed, it has acted as a conduit for rainwater. Moisture seeps down and collects in a water table, sealed underneath by the old sunken rock.

True artesian water bubbles up under its own pressure if the saturated layer is breached. But bore-sinking for almost a century has lowered the water table; pumping is often needed now. The water is increasingly salty as it ages, and it can have a sulphurous, rotten-egg smell. Most of it is used only for livestock. Where it is pumped from great depths it comes up near-boiling, and can be piped for heating.

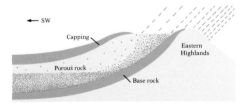

Spongy rock exposed near the Great Divide is sandwiched between layers that water cannot penetrate. Rain sinking into it forms a water table extending more than 1500 km southwestward.

Vast floodplains border the Daly River, NT

A VICTORY FOR THE WETLANDS

HUNDREDS of wildlife species rely on shallow inland waters for at least part of each year. Without swamps and marshes, many would be poorly distributed – and some extinct. But the shrinking wetlands remain targets for reclamation or water diversion.

The trend has been reversed in central NSW, where the Macquarie River spreads into 40 000 ha of meandering creeks and reedy marshes west of Coonamble. The marshes are breeding grounds particularly for ibises, along with more than 150 other species of birds and scores of different amphibians, reptiles and fish.

Upstream, the Burrendong Dam regulates the river. After 1969 the flow was sharply reduced while much of the water went to farms. The river petered out in the marshes, which were impoverished year by year.

Early in the 1980s, a proposed expansion of cotton planting called for even more water to be taken off for irrigation. Protesting conservationists were supported by wheatgrowers and graziers, who had learned that the ibis is a major predator of insects that ruin crops and pastures. The state government heeded their call.

Now the flow to the Macquarie Marshes is almost trebled. Waterfowl habitats are fully flooded, and the river can resume its natural course into the Barwon and on into the Lachlan-Darling-Murray system. The marshes, partly declared as nature reserves and listed by the Heritage Commission, are the likely site of a future national park.

Their waters restored, the Macquarie Marshes come back to life

Left: The last run-off from the summer wet season in the Kimberleys, WA, spills into the Prince Regent River. It flows straight for 80 km along a sandstone fracture

Unspoilt waterways meander through The Lakes National Park, Vic, within easy boating distance of popular Gippsland holiday resorts. The lakes were formed out of estuaries, barred by Ninety Mile Beach

Where the oceans hold sway

To SEE ALL of Australia's shores at first hand could take a lifetime – or perhaps cost a life. The mainland and Tasmanian coasts, by the most precise measuring method available, extend for more than 30 000 km. Islands on the continental shelf add nearly 18 000 km. Some sections consist of virtually impassable terrain, so far surveyed only from aircraft or boats. Fresh water may not be found for hundreds of kilometres, and the only source of food may be dangerous swamps or seas.

No other country has a coastline so vast, or so pronounced in its contrasts. Shores are backed in some places by deserts, in others by jungles. Towering cliffs and headlands offer seascapes of grandeur; elsewhere the only view may be of mudflats, all the way to the horizon. Ocean currents range from equatorial to subpolar. While seals and Antarctic seabirds breed in the south, warmer waters foster the growth of the world's most massive coral structures.

Australia's coast is noticeably lacking in one respect: for its size, it has very few river outlets. And except near the Eastern Highlands and in the monsoonal north and northwest, rivers have no significant impact on shore formations. There is simply not enough run-off of water or eroded inland rock. Disparity in the supply of material from the hinterland to the coasts, established over millions of years, has led to marked differences in the composition and behaviour of shorelines.

Where plenty of inland material is added to coastal debris, sands are abundant. But they may not stay put. They contain a lot of silica, usually in the form of quartz, so they are slippery. Agitated by waves and winds, they sort themselves until the heaviest minerals – the 'black sands' prized for commercial extraction

Coral backs WA's Houtman Abrolhos Islands – once coastal dunes but now 60 km offshore

Right: Lime-rich dunes on the Bight near Penong, SA

– lie at the bottom of beaches and dunes. Sands above are light, loose and easily torn away by gales and storm waves.

On arid shores, sands are composed more of marine sediments. Their higher content of shell and skeleton fragments makes them rich in calcium – a binding agent. Blown inland, these sands pile up and consolidate. Many wave-eroded limestone cliffs, reefs and offshore stacks originated as calcified dune ridges, built when the sea level was lower.

Not all parts of the coast are being eroded. Some hold their own against the sea, or even gain ground. Normal wave power is far from uniform around Australia. It is determined by global weather patterns and the breadth and slope of the continental shelf offshore, as well as by local geography. Waves are generally strongest in the south and ineffectual on tropical shores – except in cyclones. In the far north, river silts discharged into quiet shallows are caught in mangroves to make new land.

Wave direction is important, especially to the fate of beaches. Strong waves breaking at an acute angle to a beach create a powerful longshore current. Washed-off sand is carried away parallel to the shoreline. Where this happens consistently, beaches are depleted and the coastline gradually recedes.

Southeasterly winds and waves attack the eastern bulge of the continent with a regularity that makes beach recession a fact of life. Foredune stabilisation and restraints on property development can stop it happening more quickly than necessary, but the process is inevitable. Sand movement up the mid-east coast has been relentless for more than 8000 years, since the sea rose after the last ice age.

The outcome, where the longshore currents weaken at last, is seen in the chain of sand islands off Brisbane, in the richly coloured cliffs north of Noosa, and finally in the huge mass of Fraser Island. Most of the material that built them originated in the Great Dividing Range, perhaps as far south as the Blue Mountains. Similar forces worked on the western seaboard; in almost a mirror image, its old limestone coast is recessed in the south and built out towards the Tropic of Capricorn.

Where strong waves consistently meet a

Silt collects in a tropical tangle

THE MANGROVE KINGDOM: LIVING WITH THE TIDES

MANGROVES are trees and shrubs of many different kinds, all adapted to daily flooding by sea water. They restrict their intake of salt by chemical action, or get rid of it through their leaves. Their seeds are spread by the tides.

Australia has nearly 50 species. Most are notable for the aerial root systems that help to anchor them in soft mud. In some, the roots have openings through which the trees breathe when their soils are saturated. Other species send up breathing pegs for metres around each tree.

On northern coasts, communities of 20 of more species form broad, dense forests up to 30 metres tall. Diversity and vigour decline farther south. Around Sydney three or four species form open stands, seldom exceeding 15 metres. In Victoria, South Australia and south of Perth there is only the grey mangrove, stunted and sparsely distributed.

Boat users and resort developers may see mangroves as nuisances. But they stabilise shorelines by trapping silt in their tangled roots. And their fallen leaves start an estuarine food chain on which marine animals – including most commercially harvested fish – depend. Each square metre of tropical mangrove forest yields about 1 kg of organic matter every year.

shore head-on, they can add to the land. They push sand in to form nearshore barriers, sometimes shutting off bays or estuaries. The lagoons that are created eventually fill with silts and windblown sands. Beaches formed of massive barriers occur frequently on the east coast between the Tropic and Wilsons Promontory, and are also found in eastern South Australia and south of Perth.

Tropical Queensland and the Northern Territory, with weaker wave action, have lower barrier beaches less obvious in their origin. Gulfs and landlocked bays in these regions tend to fill as tidal mudflats, backed by broad mangrove beds and salt marshes and sometimes fringed with coral. Open tidal plains, reaching for many kilometres between high and low waterlines, occur widely on each side of North West Cape between Shark Bay and Port Hedland.

Long, open mainland beaches, free of barriers, develop where the general direction of waves is past a shoreline rather than at it. Reefs and rocky sections may give protection, but the sandy stretches predominate. They are common in western Victoria and northern and eastern Tasmania, towards the head of the Bight and in some parts of the southwest.

Headlands interrupt most beach coasts in the southeast, giving shelter and good vantage points. Their bases usually have wave-cut shore platforms, teeming with marine life. Continuously cliffed coasts, however, are rare. The principal ones in accessible areas are immediately south of Sydney – through Royal National Park and beyond – in Otway and Port Campbell National Parks in Victoria, and around most of southeastern Tasmania.

Sheer limestone cliffs give a sharp edge to much of the Nullarbor Plain, and to the desolate western extremity of the continent, north of Kalbarri National Park. The longest rock coast of all skirts the Kimberleys, where red sandstone precipices are cut by fiordlike inlets. Prodigious tides that can range up to 12 metres create channelled currents of freakish violence. And tidal bores – waves that race up rivers – can overturn boats 50 km inland.

Often it is the reefs and islands offshore that most distinguish a coast. They enrich its scenic variety, and give sanctuary to animals and plants rarely seen on the mainland. In spite of Australia's extreme emphasis on seaboard settlement and maritime recreation, landing problems and a lack of fresh water saved many islands. Now an impressive number are fully protected as nature reserves. Others rank among our most celebrated national parks.

Remote island parks, with a controlled flow of visitors, are easily managed. But on closer islands — especially the Queensland islands with fringing coral — the risks of damage are high. The jeopardy of the reef at Green Island, off Cairns, prompted a marine park declaration. That concept of below-the-waterline protection is now applied in defence of almost all of the Great Barrier Reef region.

A scalloped beach line, seen strikingly at Safety Cove on Tasman Peninsula, Tas, results when incoming and receding waves collide and set up an eddying pattern. On a surfing beach, it may indicate dangerous rip currents

The Drum and Drumsticks, off Beecroft Peninsula, NSW, are remnants of an older coastline

The eternal battle of the trees

PLANTS CANNOT RUN from hostile conditions. To survive, they must adapt and diversify. In Australia they have answered with an explosion of species. Flowering plants alone number about 11 000 kinds, from tiny herbs to towering eucalypts. Mosses, ferns, fungi and cone-bearing

trees add to the array. And rivalry is intense. Plants struggle not only against climatic setbacks, animal appetites and human ambitions, but also against one another.

The story of land vegetation starts well over 400 million years ago. Leafless, branching strands of a mossy seaweed crept ashore from the intertidal zone and invaded swamps and marshes. Adapting to more and more exposure to the air, the plants evolved into mosses and colonised firm ground.

Root systems were developed to tap subsurface water. Plants with thick, rigid stems appeared – the ancestors of ferns, club-mosses and horsetails. Competing for light, they reached up on ever-stronger trunks and became the first trees. Forests grew widely, dominated by club-mosses 30 metres tall. Coal deposits are their petrified remains.

Next, more than 250 million years ago, came the conifers – pine trees and their relatives. They broke away from reliance on ground water to disperse reproductive spores; their pollen is produced high in the tree, to be scattered by winds. Another cone-bearing group, short-trunked cycads with palmlike or fernlike fronds, appeared at about the same time. Pines and cycads ruled until 80-90 million years ago.

Flowering plants were taking over by then, especially in warmer climates. Their vivid petals, alluring scents and nectar drew insects, ensuring a more effective transfer of pollen. Magnolias and figs were among the pioneers, and beeches gained early prominence in forests. Palms were soon abundant, and took many forms. The striking thing about the flowering plants was how quickly they produced variations to suit different soils and climates.

The realm of the conifers had been worldwide. But continental isolation was setting in when flowering plants came to the fore. Africa had separated from the southern supercontinent of Gondwanaland, and India and South America were in the process of breaking away. After New Zealand drifted off, about 80 million years ago, Australia's only neighbour – and source of new plants – was Antarctica.

In the last phase of separation, some 60 million years ago, southern Australia and Antarctica shared cool-climate rainforests. Conifers still predominated, among an increasing variety of flowering trees including some beeches. Almost nothing is known of the vegetation of inland and northern Australia, but it can be assumed that the forerunners of nearly all of today's species were established. The only important exceptions, in the far north, came much later from Asia through New Guinea.

Australia's breach with Antarctica was completed about 55 million years ago. The continent began its journey northwestward into warmer latitudes. But world temperatures generally were falling, and patterns of atmospheric circulation changing. Land upheavals and sea incursions modified climates and soils in the east and south. Browsing and grazing mammals and seed-eating birds spread. But plant evolution went on. Now in isolation, it took paths that were to create a uniquely Australian bush.

With the first uplift of the Eastern Highlands completed, about 45 million years ago, beech rainforests entered a long period of dominance

Pencil pine grows only in alpine Tasmania

BUILT BY PRIMITIVE PLANTS

CLUMPS like soft rock jut from sand and mud at Hamelin Pool, a shallow arm of Shark Bay, WA. In deeper water they stand in columns up to 3 metres tall. Found in thousands, these are living colonies of single-celled plants bound by secretions of lime.

The microscopic plants, called cyanophytes, represent the earliest form of life after bacteria – and the first to put oxygen into the air. They grow commonly in mats, like algae, and are usually grazed by molluscs. Only at Hamelin Pool are they left alone to build. The outlet is choked, and high evaporation makes the water too salty for molluscs.

Shorn-off cyanophyte mounds, solidified in silica, are found as big white rings in ancient rocks all over the world. Before their organic origin was known they were named stromatolites – 'mattress stones'. Some were built by plants growing 3000 million years ago.

Oddities of western and northern WA: Millstream palms (left) and baobabs or bottle trees – called boabs by locals

at least in the south. The general climate was still moist, but the interior of the continent was already more arid. And plants there were adapting. Trees that had emerged in luxury, enjoying abundant rainfall and rich soils, differentiated to include hardier forms.

Out of the acacia family – the wattles – came an exclusively Australian type with flattened, thornlike stems instead of leaves. From the myrtles, which in tropical America bear a soft, pulpy fruit, came eucalypts with tough, woody capsules. Both groups are thought to have gained some prominence in open forests by 30 million years ago. They and many other flowering trees continued to vary, developing scrubbier forms to survive in the poorest soils.

No one knows when the first alien plants may have arrived, their seeds carried by ocean currents or migratory birds. But intermittently over the past 10 million years, since Australia came into close contact with New Guinea, invaders of Southeast Asian origin have travelled overland. They established themselves with particular success in northern rainforests.

In most of the south, also about 10 million years ago, beech forests suddenly gave way to eucalypts. Some open woodlands and grasslands appeared, though their major expansion did not occur until 3-1 million years ago. By then the world was entering a period – continuing now – in which the climate fluctuated in cycles of glaciation and heating.

Trees advanced or retreated according to their resistance to frost, heat and drought – and increasingly to fire. Expanding populations of browsing animals chewed at them. Through it all, the grasses gained ground. They carpeted alpine plateaux and semi-arid plains, and clung in hummocks in places so barren that not even the scrub eucalypts and acacias could survive.

In a climate steadily more arid, rainforests

Cycads ruled for eons before palms evolved

were forced back to the eastern margins of the continent about 2 million years ago. Since then, in patches within those limits, they have contracted and expanded many times in a to-and-fro struggle with dry-adapted trees. And in tropical rainforests, the component plants have fought among themselves. Different species show up during each phase of resurgence, in fossils taken from the same spot.

Fire has been a powerful influence on Australian plant evolution for many millions of years. The fact that so many species benefit from burning and some even rely on it is evidence of that. But charcoal deposits and soil studies show a marked increase in the frequency of fires – and the expansion of grasslands – in the past 40 000 years.

Aborigines used fire to foster the wildlife they hunted. Blazes were started judiciously to keep woodlands clear of litter and encourage grass growth – not too often, yet not so seldom that huge conflagrations were caused. But European settlers anxious for agricultural land burned forests, woodlands and scrublands indiscriminately, and their raging fires bared far more ground than was needed.

Rainforest logging, the substitution of exotic plantations and the spread of introduced pasture grasses and farm crops have all had an obvious impact on native vegetation. More subtle is the conversion of soils by compaction under the hooves of thousands of millions of livestock. Often the bush is damaged by feral animals such as goats and pigs, or supplanted by alien trees and weeds. But on the vast scale of plant evolution, all these are just further complications – and perhaps passing phases – in a battle that never ends.

Rainforests: a squandered heritage

Scores of tree species vie for space and light in the one small patch of tropical rainforest

RAINFORESTS are the scattered relics of an ancient time when most of Australia was moist and fertile. Driven back by a drying climate, they were overtaken by trees better able to resist drought and fire. Before Europeans came, the domain of rainforests was reduced already to less than 1 per cent of the continent's area. Now it is barely a quarter of that. In the main, whatever was most accessible has gone.

Generations of loggers and farmers who felled or burned the trees were largely ignorant of the consequences. They did not realise the extent to which they would trigger off soil erosion and the loss of water yields. They could not foresee a day when the forests would be needed to purify a polluted atmosphere. Least of all could they have understood that they were depleting a genetic store in which some stock – perhaps unseen – might be unique.

Even today it is not always grasped that rainforest species are interdependent. A certain tree may be widely distributed, so its removal from one forest seems harmless. But that could spell the doom of other plants whose habitat is more limited. Simply letting too much light in can kill many species. They may be merely fungi or mosses of no apparent significance. But they could have undiscovered properties important to human survival.

Shade – not just wetness or the types of trees – makes a rainforest. The leaves of the taller trees intermingle to form a canopy. By most botanical definitions, rainforests are at least 70 per cent enclosed under their canopies. Some are totally closed: treetops cannot be seen from the ground, and any light is filtered. Such forests are so humid that hot weather is intolerable – and so dark that walkers may be unable to see hazards.

Left alone, a rainforest recycles the mineral nutrients in dead trees and other fallen material. Decay is so rapid that the soil need not be especially fertile – nearly all the nutrients are stored above ground. But if erosion strips off the litter, or it is burnt and the ash washes away, the forest starves. So the local occurrence of rainforests is related not only to rainfall reliability but also to the least likelihood of fire. Even where eucalypts have come to rule, pockets of rainforest survive in protected gorges and gullies.

Tasmania has the most extensive rainforests – cool spreads of myrtle beech richly carpeted with mosses and ferns. They also occur in limited areas of Victoria. Stands of the closely related negrohead beech occupy high ranges in northern NSW and southern Queensland. Ancestors of these beeches were established before the southern supercontinent of Gondwanaland broke up: kindred trees grow in New Zealand and Chile and are fossillised in Antarctica. Later, beeches were probably the commonest forest trees in most of Australia.

Beech forests are simple in composition. Mature stands grow to a uniform height and have no understoreys made up of other tree species. Tree ferns may grow luxuriantly where the canopy is more open – particularly along riverbanks. But the forest floors are mainly mossy. Epiphytes – plants that attach themselves to others – and parasites, which feed off

Left: Cool-temperate forests of myrtle beech grow widely in Tasmania and in patches in Victoria – such as this one in Wilsons Promontory National Park. Tree ferns abound where the canopy opens along rivers

Negrohead beech, the ruler of temperate rainforests, nears the northern end of its range in Nightcap National Park, NSW

others, are few except for lichens. The beeches may grow to 30 metres, but in the coldest conditions do not exceed 10 metres.

Northern rainforests are much more complex. More than 100 different tree species may be found in one hectare, and none is noticeably dominant. The general height of the canopy is usually 30 metres or so, but here and there an emergent tree stands much taller. And below the canopy are understoreys of shorter trees. Vines climb towards the light, and epiphytes such as orchids and staghorn and elkhorn ferns are abundant. But the forest floor is surprisingly open. Palms and ferns grow fairly sparsely among fleshy-leafed herbs and a few small shrubs and tree seedlings. These seedlings seem never to get any taller – but if adult trees come down, through old age or storm damage, the opening of the canopy brings them shooting up to fill the gap.

Lichen-covered and nearly always buttressed at their bases, the different northern trees are hard to tell apart at ground level. Prized timber species surviving in remote forests include red cedar, coachwood, silky oak, Queensland maple and teak and the imposing kauri, which reaches 50 metres. This great pine, with relatives in New Zealand and New Caledonia, has a lineage even older than the beeches. The northern forests are equally a part of the Gondwanaland legacy.

Forests in the far north have been enriched more recently, however, by Asiatic plants arriving through New Guinea. That heightens a distinction often made between tropical and subtropical northern rainforests. The first kind contain many more species. But the division has nothing to do with the line of the Tropic of Capricorn – it relates to temperature ranges and altitude. Tropical forests in this sense are not found south of Townsville, and even to the north they are replaced by subtropical mixtures in the higher country.

The northern half of Cape York Peninsula has part-time rainforests. Plants here have to cope with months of drought between monsoons. So the forests are dominated by deciduous species that conserve moisture by shedding their leaves at the onset of the dry season. Since roads are open only in the 'Dry', most travellers do not recognise the rainforests. Small patches of similar vegetation occur in the Darwin region, where they are more often called monsoon vineforests.

Beyond their scenic value and their importance as botanical storehouses, rainforests are the busiest havens of wildlife on land. They seethe with the activities of myriads of creatures, at every level from the leaf litter to the topmost flower heads. Rare insects, amphibians, mammals and birds are among the occupants. Whatever threatens rainforests may ring the death knell of these animals.

Starting life as seeds lodged high in other tropical trees, curtain figs send down prop roots – then strangle their hosts

THE PARKS WHERE RAINFORESTS RULE

POCKETS of rainforest are found in the majority of eastern national parks. Those areas with a significant amount of rainforest include:

Cairns region Barron Gorge, Bellenden Ker, Cape Tribulation, Clump Mountain (Maria Creek group), Daintree, Dunk Island, Ella Bay, Graham Range, Green Island, Grey Peaks, Iron Range, Lake Barrine, Lake Eacham, Lizard Island, Mount Hypipamee, Palmerston group, Topaz Road, Tully Gorge.

Townsville region Conway, Eungella, Goold Island (Hinchinbrook Island group), Jourama, Lumholtz, Mount Jukes (Mount Blackwood group), Mount Spec, Orpheus Island, Whitsunday Island.

Rockhampton region Cape Palmerston, Coalstoun Lakes, Fairlies Knob (Mount Walsh group), Kroombit Tops, Mount Bauple, Northumberland Islands.

Brisbane region Bunya Mountains, Burleigh Head, Conondale, Lamington, Maiala (D'Aguilar Range group), Main Range, Springbrook, Tamborine Mountain group, The Palms.

NSW northern border region Border Ranges, Dorrigo, Gibraltar Range, Mount Warning, New England, Nightcap, Washpool

Melbourne region Alfred, Tarra-Bulga, Croajingolong, Mitchell River, Otway, Wilsons Promontory.

Tasmania Cradle Mountain-Lake St Clair, Mount Field, Southwest, Walls of Jerusalem, Franklin-Gordon Wild Rivers.

The forests that welcome fire

TREES MEET nature's harshest terms in Australia's open forests and woodlands. They face the certainty of wildfire. Many have adapted so that they can recover after burning. And some – particularly the eucalypts – now depend on fire for their procreation. They give typical 'gum tree' bushland not only its own look but even its own smell: evaporating oils.

Long before humans arrived to step up the pace of destruction, fires occurred naturally. Lightning strikes were most often the cause. The trees that stood the best chance were those with lignotubers – swellings near the base of the trunk containing latent buds. These come to life if the tree is damaged above. In some species lignotubers are seen as warty lumps on the trunk. But many Australian trees have them underground, extending much like roots.

Eucalypts and some of their companion trees in the open forests developed further defences. They enclosed their seeds in woody cases instead of soft fruits, and many acquired unusually thick bark. But the most successful species went beyond mere survival – they found ways of exploiting fire for their own benefit. They made sure that when a forest was burnt out, it was replaced by their offspring rather than an invading species. Evolution has brought some eucalypts to a point at which, once at least in their seed-bearing lives, they *need* burning down.

The tallest and fastest-growing eucalypts occupy high-rainfall districts. But they rely on strong light. If an overgrown forest becomes too shady, eucalypt seedlings are killed by fungi. Such a forest is waiting for a dry spell followed by a hot, fast-moving fire. Then, at the height of its destruction, it re-seeds itself.

Fed by streamers of peeling bark, flames race up the trunks to the forest canopy. Vaporised leaf oil ignites – sometimes it explodes – drawing the fire even more quickly away from the ground and through the canopy. And from under the vanishing foliage pours a shower of seed capsules – the output of not just one season, but perhaps three or four.

If the fire has moved on quickly enough the seeds are undamaged. (In a furnace test, green capsules protected their seeds for 9 minutes at 440°C.) Germination starts in a bed of ash, holding mineral nutrients in a form that the seedlings can most readily absorb. Their growth is astonishing: some saplings gain 5 metres in a year. In a burnt eucalypt forest, trees of other families have no chance of taking over.

Tall open forests – referred to in older books as wet hardleaf or wet sclerophyll forests – are at their most grand in the extreme southeast and southwest. In Tasmania and Victoria they include the world's tallest hardwood, mountain ash *Eucalyptus regnans*, which can exceed

100 metres. In Western Australia the karri *Eucalyptus diversicolor*, only slightly shorter, is king. Alpine ash, brown stringybark, blackbutt and blue gum are prominent in NSW, and rose gum is characteristic around Brisbane.

These forests are more open at the top than rainforests – canopy coverage is 30-70 per cent – but much leafier below. There is always a dense understorey of shorter eucalypt species and taller shrubs. On rich soils in the moistest areas, some of the understorey plants are rainforest species – on the way to taking over if fire does not come. With tree ferns, lichens and epiphytes abundant, some wet open forests at ground level look much like rainforests. But the trunk bases are not buttressed.

The dominion of eucalypts continues in drier open forests in southern Australia but the trees seldom exceed 30 metres. Fires are more frequent and most species are adapted to resist, then recover through lignotubers. Understoreys are less leafy, with acacias, casuarinas and banksias usually prominent. The most characteristic eucalypt species include peppermint, bloodwood, scribbly gum, stringybark and 'apple' (angophora) in the southeast, and

Heartwood fire dooms a tree – but its scattered seeds and underground tubers are intact

Damage higher up triggers new growth from a charred trunk

Left: A handsome stand of marri, with an understorey of karri oak, in WA's Walpole-Nornalup National Park. Marri grows widely in the southwest where it reaches heights of 30-40 metres. It shares the same range as jarrah and karri and often occurs with them. Its timber does not compare with that of the other two hardwoods – it is marred by gum pockets and rings

COUNTLESS diseases and pests attack eucalypts – especially where natural balances are disrupted. If large numbers of trees are slowly dying, their decline is generally labelled 'dieback'. It is not one problem but many, with different causes.

A soil-borne fungus attacks the giant jarrahs of Western Australia. To limit its spread some state forest areas and national parks are quarantined; there are wash-down facilities to prevent vehicles carrying infected soil from one area to another; road construction and use are restricted.

Dieback in irrigation areas (particularly in the Murray-Murrumbidgee Basin) occurs because of salting and an altered water table: too much water prevents soil aeration and rots tree roots; too little and the trees die of thirst.

Leaf-eating Christmas beetles and other insects are a major cause of eucalypt dieback in the New England district of NSW. Development of pastoral agriculture has provided more food for the beetles' larval stage while removing farmland trees so there are fewer birds to eat increasing numbers of beetles.

River red gum dieback in northwestern Victoria

In the Dandenong Ranges near Melbourne, the problem seems to be too many birds. Dieback has occurred in about 10 per cent of the forest cover because of an infestation by sap-sucking insects called psyllids. These are husbanded by a big population of bellbirds, which eat only the older psyllids and encourage the young to develop. Other birds with less selective appetites are driven away.

messmate, boxes and pink gum near Adelaide. The Perth region has its own group, dominated by jarrah, marri and wandoo.

Casuarinas and acacias rule in many open forests in Queensland, between hoop pine on the wetter seaward margins and cypress pine at the inland limit of forest growth. There are also some eucalypt forests, with grassy floors suggesting that they gained their hold through firing by Aboriginal hunters. Similar grassy eucalypt forests occur in the Darwin region and the Kimberleys, and along the Murray River Valley where they are dominated by the flood-loving river red gum.

Woodlands are distinguished from forests by having a canopy coverage of less than 30 per cent of their area. Often they are simply extensions of forest communities, more widely spaced because they have less soil moisture to share. Grasses are much more common, however. And some non-eucalypt species – melaleucas (paperbarks), for example – take on a prominence not seen in forests. Brigalow, once the most significant of woodland acacias, exists now only in remnants on its range from inland mid-Queensland to northern NSW.

In woodlands as much as in forests, eucalypts remain the most widespread and dominant trees. Their forms range from the snow gums of alpine summits to monsoon species that shed their leaves for the 'Dry'. Counting the stunted types of the outback, there may be more than 500 eucalypt species; botanists are forever making new finds and classifications,

Tree ferns are characteristic of the cooler wet eucalypt forests of the southeast – but never found in those of the west

and raising or lowering the figure. However many there are, eucalypts represent the plant kingdom's greatest evolutionary triumph – a conquest of every climatic extreme that the continent can offer.

But the unmistakable aroma of 'gum' leaves, and the blue haze pervading forests in hot weather, are reminders of menace. The layers of oily foliage and the thickly littered floors are incendiary bombs, certain sooner or later to go off. Eucalypts and many of their companions have accommodated to an element against which humans are largely helpless. Fire is a fact of their lives.

Sentinels of the never-never

SCRUB, SPINIFEX and saltbush ... half of Australia is dismissed in three words. Yet in some ways the vegetation of the scorched, parched outback is the most important of all. It sustained the spread of Aboriginal tribes. It afforded the food, shelter and fuel to make the continent traversable – if seldom habitable – by Europeans and their livestock. And in spite of these intrusions, it has ensured the survival of many wildlife species.

Hardly any of the hinterland is absolute desert. Almost anywhere something grows, to make up the world's greatest array of dry-living plants. But two groups of stunted trees, mulga and mallee, have a hold so persistent that their habitats take their names. The Mulga is an immense tract of acacia scrub and sparse shrubland sweeping across Western Australia into the Northern Territory and South Australia, with outliers to the east. The Mallee's parched plains span southwestern NSW, northwestern Victoria and eastern South Australia. Even more mallee country extends west of Adelaide and round the Great Australian Bight to beyond Kalgoorlie, WA.

Mulga denotes one main wattle species, *Acacia aneura*, which on the best soils can reach 15 metres but in its shrub form can be as low as 2 metres. Its many branches, rising steeply from the ground or just above, carry slightly flattened stems – called phyllodes – instead of leaves. These have a hairy, resinous covering and point skyward to minimise heating. Trees go dormant in drought, but revive within four days of receiving moisture in their soil. They do best where there is some chance of rain at any time of year; in regions of strongly seasonal rainfall they tend to be replaced by casuarinas – the so-called oaks.

Aboriginal boomerangs and many souvenir ornaments are made of mulga wood. Livestock prefer browsing the phyllodes – though they are not particularly nutritious – to eating dry grass. Mulga is harvested as emergency fodder in droughts, and sometimes cleared where there is an understorey of edible tussock grasses. But the trees are secure in the driest areas, and where their understoreys are of inedible small shrubs or hummock grasses.

Mallees are ground-branching eucalypts. More than 100 species have been identified. They form a spreading bush, usually 3-9 metres tall, from an underground lignotuber that contains latent buds to regenerate the tree if it is damaged. Six months after a fire, they may have produced up to 70 new shoots. Stem branches are few and leaves are borne only at the tips of the branches. In dense scrub they form a distinctive canopy cover, shallow and almost horizontal.

Since drought-resistant wheat strains were developed, extensive mallee areas have been cleared – with some calamitous consequences. Without the cover of the mallees and their understorey shrubs and grasses, strong winds after long dry spells can rip all of the topsoil away. Millions of tonnes of red dust are dumped in choking storms on towns and cities or into the oceans; some is even blown as far as New Zealand.

On limy or salty soils, both mulga and mallee may merge into country dominated by low chenopod shrubs – saltbushes and their relatives. They are palatable to stock, and when agriculture invaded the outback their territories were the easiest to take. Saltbushes decline with years of grazing: of about 250 chenopod species, more than 20 are expected to disappear from the wild by the end of the century. But the others hold about 6 per cent of the mainland area. Most are in inland South Australia and on the Nullarbor Plain, with an isolated stronghold in western NSW around the dried-out Willandra Lakes.

Spiky hummock grasses dot arid land over a quarter of the continent, from the northwest coast into Queensland and south almost to the Nullarbor. Mostly species of *Triodia*, they are usually called spinifex – though true *Spinifex* exists as a coastal sand-binding plant. To avoid confusion some people call the inland hummock type porcupine grass. It normally occurs in mulga scrub or casuarina woodlands, but on rocky slopes and sandplains it may provide the only ground cover.

Open grasslands of softer, edible tussocks such as Mitchell grass range from south of Arnhem Land and the Gulf of Carpentaria to southwestern Queensland. But most are heavily grazed. Untouched grasslands now are vir-

Spinifex and snappy gums on the Hamersley Range, WA

Poached-egg daisies: the waiting is over

PLANTS THAT HIDE FROM DROUGHT

RAIN in late winter changes the look of arid inland regions with remarkable speed. Unseen in the ground are seeds that can bide their time through years of drought. When conditions favour them they burst into hectic life. Plants shoot in hours and flower in days. Almost as quickly they wither and die, leaving a new generation of seeds to wait once more.

Most such plants – called ephemerals – are members of the daisy or pea families. Their seeds are programmed so as not to be fooled by a passing shower, or by heavier rain at the wrong time of year. As well as searing heat, frost must be avoided. Germination is triggered only by a certain combination of moisture, temperature and light intensity.

Ephemerals have their easiest life near rock outcrops, where they may flourish annually in pockets of run-off moisture. In Central Australia, the seepage of dew from sealed, high-crowned highways is sometimes enough to promote growth along a narrow band at each side. But the most spectacular shows follow heavy rains on flat country. Drab tonings turn green, then explode into vivid colours as far as the eye can see.

Hops and everlastings make the most of run-off

but most do not need to. Their seeds are distributed whenever they are ready – by harvester ants. These seeds all have a tough casing but they bear a soft tail. The ants carry the seeds to their nests, eat the tail, then discard the seeds undamaged. Sometimes they store them in underground galleries. Some 1500 Australian plant species use ants in this fashion, compared with fewer than 300 anywhere else in the world.

Heathlands in the east and south are generally small patches, merging into scrub or woodlands. Most are coastal, on sandy soils. But highland heaths occur in parts of the Great Dividing Range – on soils derived from sandstone or granite – and in Tasmania. In the west, immense tracts of heathland reach east from Albany and north from Kalbarri – not merely along the coast but also on sandplains well inland. It is their predominance that gives Western Australia its well-justified reputation as 'the wildflower state'.

Left: Mallees and pearl bluebush – a kind of saltbush – merge on the sandplains of Nullarbor National Park, SA. Feral camels are often seen

Below: Scrubs at Wyperfeld National Park, Vic, support at least 200 native bird species

tually confined to very wet areas – the high buttongrass plains of southwestern Tasmania, for example, or the swampgrass plains near parts of the NSW south coast.

Heathland plants make up the remainder of the vegetation of the wide-open spaces. In their domain, forest growth is ruled out not by aridity but by soil infertility. In compensation, the flowering shrubs of the heathlands present the most vivid scenes of the bush, and support a profusion of wildlife. Birds such as honeyeaters and parrots are likeliest to catch the eye, but smaller marsupials also feed on nectar and on the insects that swarm in the undergrowth.

Australia's main family of true heaths, the epacrids, has more than 300 species. The best known, common heath with its dangling tubular flowers borne year-round, is Victoria's floral emblem. Lilies and their relatives grow mostly as heath plants, along with thousands of smaller flowering species including ground orchids in a rich variety of forms and colours. But they and the true heaths are dominated by mixtures of taller woody shrubs. The most characteristic family, the proteaceae, includes banksias, grevilleas, hakeas, waratahs and Western Australia's dryandras. Small eucalypts, acacias, paperbarks, tea-trees and casuarinas are also common – but often the most distinctive plants of heathlands are grass trees.

Nearly all species on the fire-prone heathlands can regenerate from underground organs. Some release seed capsules during a fire,

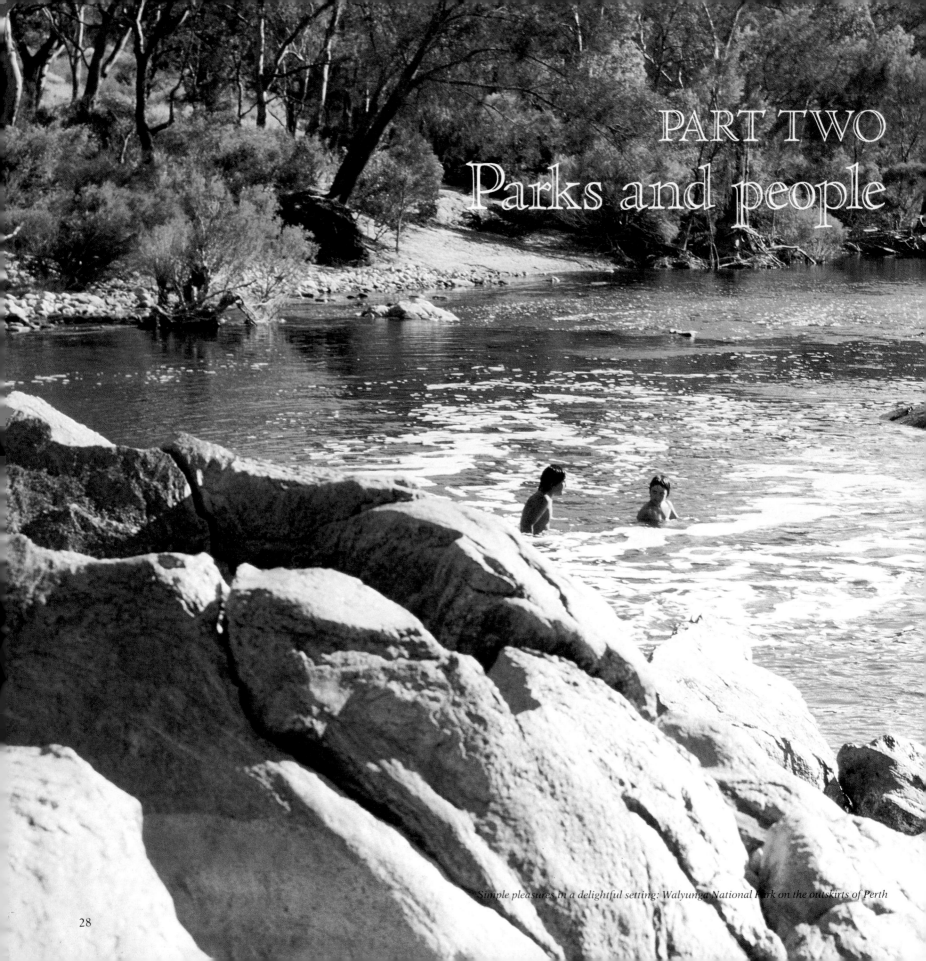

PART TWO
Parks and people

Simple pleasures in a delightful setting: Walyunga National Park on the outskirts of Perth

28

Running a national park is a balancing act – protecting the environment while letting people enjoy it. Each place has its special problems, with dedicated rangers and backroom staff working to solve them. But a great deal more is up to the public.

29

Why we have national parks

TAXPAYERS' MONEY goes into national parks, so people are entitled to see some return for it. Where parks provide recreational opportunities close to cities, or where they preserve unusually spectacular scenery, the benefits are clear. The value of protecting wildlife habitats is also widely recognised at last. But in an increasing number of cases, the worth of new parks is far from obvious to the public.

Some are dedicated in places that no one but a scientist would dream of visiting. Western Australia's vast Rudall River National Park, for example, covers a forbidding expanse of rock ridges and dunes between the Gibson and Great Sandy Deserts. It has no roads, and seldom any water. Many parks are sited in high country so rugged that it is penetrated only by expert climbers. Others occupy monotonous stretches of scrub or swampland, offering nothing noteworthy to see or do.

Public benefits are derived in indirect and sometimes unexpected ways. The real importance of a high, forested park may lie in ensuring the adequacy and purity of water supplies to a nearby community. Even without rain, trees shed more moisture than they receive from the air. And they combat air pollution.

Apart from the varying scenic and recreational merits of national parks, and their role in the protection of the environment and wildlife, they can offer four other advantages from which the whole community stands to gain:

Education Field studies by school groups and trainee teachers are given active assistance. Junior ranger programmes encourage children to follow nature interests in their spare time. Advice by parks staff is also offered in courses for private landowners.

Scientific research Professional studies and experiments are permitted in national parks if

Scientists are still exploring at Rudall River, WA. The public's turn will come much later

they cannot be mounted elsewhere and are not unduly destructive. Untouched areas also serve as models, against which scientists can measure what happens when similar environments outside the parks are interfered with.

Biological banks Without park protection, many plants and animals would no longer exist. Their genetic combinations would be lost to the world. So would the possibility of using them to develop new medicines, food sources and industrial techniques.

Foreign income The fame of many of Australia's national parks is a powerful magnet to overseas visitors. And a major export earner, the fishing industry, depends on the protection of estuarine and island breeding grounds.

If planners had unlimited funds, they would provide many more parks. In the meantime, where population pressures are intense, they encourage passive recreation. They want visitors to relax, look and listen, rather than seek too many artificial amenities and active pastimes. Popular enjoyment has to be balanced

against the fragility of natural environments – or else there may be nothing to enjoy later on.

Park administrations bear a responsibility to future generations, not only in Australia but also throughout the world. Our parks and wildlife services belong to an international union, formed under United Nations auspices, and the federal and state governments endorse all of its ideals. But we struggle to live up to them.

The international convention calls for national parks and nature reserves to make up at least 5 per cent of any country's territory. Australia, in spite of many recent additions, falls far short. And the parks are meant to represent every kind of biological community. Again Australia fails: virtually all temperate and subtropical grasslands, for example, have long been transformed by livestock.

Scarcity of land puts environmental aims in conflict with industrial interests. Remaining areas suitable for parks are often earmarked for mining or logging or hydro-electricity generation. Political pressures to continue indus-

Schoolchildren find an easy introduction to nature study at Ferntree Gully National Park, Vic

trial activity, at least for a time, are usually intense. Sometimes a mixture of uses seems entirely reasonable. But the international agreement requires a nation's 'highest competent authority' to eliminate any exploitation in national parks.

Australia's trouble has been that the highest authority, the federal government, holds absolute power only in Commonwealth territories – the ACT, the Northern Territory, Jervis Bay and some remote oceanic islands. Elsewhere, the federal system gives state governments the right to declare their own reserves and dispose of them as they please. Their older 'national'

parks were created under diverse political influences to achieve different goals. Nationwide concerns were never paramount – let alone international responsibilities.

Dissension over such issues as uranium mining, oil prospecting and civil engineering continues to make political battlegrounds of some present and proposed national parks. But in management techniques and planning, at least, Canberra and the states are now in closer accord. Since the mid-1970s all legislatures have passed national parks and wildlife acts along broadly similar lines. Under a council of all the ministers with nature conservation re-

sponsibilities, senior officials of the various parks services form a standing committee to co-ordinate policies.

All of Australia's governments today have the benefit of the same high grade of professional advice on nature conservation, considered in the full light of national need. None of them wishes to be seen as environmentally irresponsible, so recommendations for new or expanded parks are usually received sympathetically. Whether enough money can be found to manage them, and provide the right balance of protection and public enjoyment, is altogether another matter.

The Royal: where it all started

Park expansion at Era took in holiday shacks – and herds of imported deer

IDEAS of nature conservation took a back seat in 1879, when Australia's first national park was conceived. The vision was not of a noble wilderness, to be kept sacred, but of a tamed and groomed playground – a Sydney version of London's Hampstead Heath.

Creation of the National Park (its only name for three-quarters of a century) was primarily a public health measure. Sydney's population had doubled in a decade: in some slums, one child in four died before it was five years old. The people needed common land.

Country to the south, cut off by the Hacking River, was about to be opened up by the Illawarra railway. Legislators reserved 7000 hectares for public recreation, and trustees hastened to meet the leisure tastes of the time. Riverside forest was hacked down to make way for lawns and European trees. Deer were brought in, and exotic birds and fish were released. A causeway controlled the river. Pavilions, guest houses and camps sprang up nearby. Cart roads and bridle paths wound into the bush. A tourist village, Audley, had its own vegetable plots, dairy pastures, orchard and blacksmith's forge.

Sports grounds were envisaged – even a horse racing track. In the meantime, undeveloped areas were cleared by the army for manoeuvres and artillery practice. And to recoup the cost of public amenities, the trustees were allowed to license grazing, logging and mining in the park.

Nature lovers were objecting before World War I, and in 1922 they successfully challenged a mining company's right to fell and mill native trees for pit props. But they could do nothing to stem the tide of cars that soon started to swamp the park. The trustees saw it as their duty to provide maximum access.

Motor roads criss-crossed the heathlands and reached the coastal cliffs and bays. People parked, picnicked, camped and cut firewood anywhere. Beach shacks appeared, and during the 1930s Depression the railway side of the park was dotted with humpies put up by jobless men. Some made livings by stealing greenery to supply city florists, or by selling cartloads of timber or soil.

Still more bush suffered in World War II, when the army set up coastal defences and used much of the park for training exercises. Postwar affluence brought a new flood of cars and motor bikes, and the first 'scrub bashers' in off-road vehicles.

The park was granted its Royal prefix in 1955, but to conservationists it seemed a lost cause. Still, it served as an object lesson, readily pointed to by professional ecologists when official policies came under fire in the next decade. After NSW set up Australia's first integrated parks and wildlife service in 1967, the professionals took charge of the mutilated old reserve and set about giving it another chance.

Cars were restricted to a few formed roads and parking zones. Ramshackle buildings were demolished. Maintenance of ornamental gardens and any other attempts to outdo nature were abandoned. The bush came back, season by season, until in its centenary year at the end of the 1970s the Royal National Park could wear its title with some pride.

Imitating an English pleasure garden suited Sydney ideas of ease in Edwardian times

Soldiers took over in World War I, baring the heathlands

Jacks and Jills of all trades

Many ranger tasks are sheer drudgery: emptying garbage bins is not the worst of them

OUTDOOR WORK in a pleasant setting … that is one part of the picture of a park ranger's life. But another may be writing reports and keeping financial records – or cleaning lavatories. Some tasks entail days and nights of utter solitude. Others require the poise and patience to deal with constant streams of people. Physical demands are high. Rangers have to be dedicated, fit and above all versatile.

Looking after the public constitutes the major part of the workload. Visitors expect easy road access and parking. They want eating facilities, campsites, piped water and sanitation – and nobody else's garbage. They seek information: signposts, leaflets, displays, advice. And they are entitled to safety. Walking routes must be secured and waterways patrolled. People astray in big parks may have to be found and helped, and perhaps given first-aid treatment. But all too often, what park visitors need most is policing.

Enforcement of regulations is the priority role of all rangers. They must keep dogs, cats and firearms out of parks, and make sure that no native plants, animals, rocks or soil are taken without licence. They must try to prevent off-road driving, and any intrusion into areas that are quarantined because plants are regenerating or endangered animals are breeding. Vitally, they have to see that fire restrictions and bans are obeyed.

Every year the parks services report hundreds of prosecutions and fines. Many other infringements are dealt with by a formal caution or just a friendly reminder – sometimes at the risk of abuse or violence. A Sydney Harbour ranger, patrolling by launch, spotted a beach party round an illicit fire. He went ashore to chide the group and was brutally bashed. Even organised crime impinges on parks: rangers in remote districts have had tense encounters with drug smugglers and marijuana growers.

Practical work to protect the environment is often sheer hard labour. Firebreaks and trails have to be maintained, and precautionary burns carried out. Most parks are at constant war with noxious weeds, feral animals or soil and sand dune erosion. Many have vandalism to contend with as well, or simply the inevitable wear and tear of heavy visiting. And parks services are increasingly taking over and trying to restore land damaged by other uses.

Rangers' reports form the basis of much of the park information that is distributed to the public. They also contribute to the resource studies and environmental impact assessments that precede major changes in management policies. Rangers may be called on for field observations to establish the numbers and movements of endangered animals, the loca-

tion of rare plants, or the rate of decay of delicate landforms. Their judgments help decide where visitors are encouraged to go and what they are encouraged to do.

Educating the public is another big role. Some rangers spend much of their time running information and display centres or conducting guided walks. School parties receive special treatment, and rangers also go to schools for classroom talks. Landholders are offered advice on soil conservation, native tree care, wildlife protection, pest control and so on. Public relations addresses are often made to community groups – including some that are opposed to national parks. Hardest to win over are farmers who fear crop raids by animals from nearby parks, local body leaders who resent the loss of ratable land, and people whose livings depend on logging or mining.

Rangers of both sexes are highly trained in emergency procedures: fire fighting, search and rescue, first aid and sometimes flood response. Often they trap or kill animals – in the far north, their tasks may include buffalo musters and crocodile shoots. But little of a ranger's work is so exciting. Much more is mundane: fixing, cleaning and improving facilities, removing refuse, spraying weeds, supervising and informing visitors, issuing permits, collecting fees, answering mail and attending to clerical details.

Carpentry skills ease a climb for nature trail parties

Winter duties in the Victorian Alps include clearing away snowdrifts so that skiers can get to their slopes – and then retrieving casualties

While tourists shun Kakadu's 'Wet', hard work goes on

Positions are so sought after, however, that the parks services can be extremely selective. They usually insist on land management experience, and some states require applicants to hold a diploma in park management, environmental studies or natural sciences. And even that does not guarantee them a job – let alone any choice in where they work. Some busy parks employ a less formally qualified grade of 'park worker', chosen usually for manual skills. But the rangers themselves are expected to be competent and self-reliant in work such as carpentry and mechanical maintenance, along with bushcraft.

Staff with the highest qualifications usually work from regional centres or state head offices. They include architects, designers, lawyers, archeologists and publications specialists. But most are science graduates and technicians, conducting biological and environmental research. A few in each state concentrate on interpretation – the evaluation and explanation of park resources – and planning. This provides the main basis of management policy, which in turn determines how the rangers in the field have to do their work.

Queensland rangers collect data for turtle research

Staying alive in the bush

FIRE IS BY FAR the greatest danger that visitors could face in national parks. When hot winds blow, bushfires can flare with little warning and approach with astonishing speed. But they move on just as quickly. Applying some commonsense safety procedures, no one need be killed or even badly burnt.

In the first place, parks consisting of eucalypt forests, dense scrub or heavily vegetated heathlands are best avoided when fire risks are extreme. They will be stiflingly hot and dusty anyway – hardly enjoyable unless they give access to rivers. Most parks display risk indicators near their entrances. And on the worst days, when total fire bans are declared, they are announced in all radio, newspaper and television weather reports. Check before setting out for a park; if there is a total ban in the district, consider changing your plans.

Fire bans are declared by statewide authorities. But park managements at any time can impose their own rules on the types of fires allowed. These are made clear on signs and in leaflets. Whichever sort of restriction applies, it is enforceable in court. Ignoring it could cost a stiff fine – even jail – or people's lives. For safety's sake alone the rules must be obeyed. And smokers have a particular responsibility to see that matches and butts are extinguished.

The killer in bushfires is not usually flame,

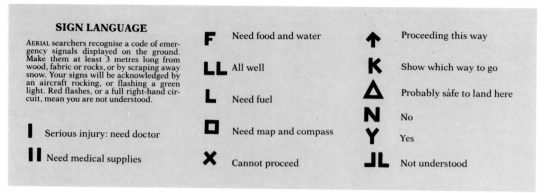

SIGN LANGUAGE

AERIAL searchers recognise a code of emergency signals displayed on the ground. Make them at least 3 metres long from wood, fabric or rocks, or by scraping away snow. Your signs will be acknowledged by an aircraft rocking, or flashing a green light. Red flashes, or a full right-hand circuit, mean you are not understood.

F Need food and water

LL All well

L Need fuel

□ Need map and compass

I Serious injury: need doctor

II Need medical supplies

X Cannot proceed

↑ Proceeding this way

K Show which way to go

△ Probably safe to land here

N No

Y Yes

⅃L Not understood

but radiated heat. Shield yourself from it. If you are on foot with a fire approaching, don't flee blindly. Look around for the best refuge – in a steep-banked creekbed, or behind a rock outcrop or a fallen log where the vegetation is thinnest. Keep low as you move – crawl if you must – to avoid smoke inhalation. If there is no shelter in sight, lie face down on a bare patch of ground. Scoop out a hollow for yourself if you can, and use loose soil to cover any exposed skin. When the main blaze has passed over you, move to where nothing is left to burn.

If you are in a car, stay there – it is your best possible shield against radiant heat. Cars are unlikely to catch fire, and sealed petrol tanks do not explode. Never try to drive through smoke. Park at the roadside – avoiding thick undergrowth and long grass – and turn on your headlights. Close windows and air vents, and block any chinks with paper or fabric. Get down on the floor and use the mats to cover exposed skin.

Bites and stings Never walk far into the bush without long trousers, socks and thick footwear. Take the greatest care where you tread on warm, sunny days, when snakes are most active. If you see a snake in your path, don't try to poke at it – annoyed in that way, it is most likely to strike. But if you stand well clear and make plenty of noise, it will go away.

Most of Australia's 140 snake species are venomous, but only about 15 are capable of killing humans. Unless you are expert in identifying species, however, regard any snakebite as dangerous. Apply a bandage that puts firm pressure *directly on the bitten area* – not a tourniquet. If a limb is bitten, immobilise it with a splint. Then quickly alert a ranger. The park may have its own venom-identification kit and anti-venom supplies.

A lethal species of funnel-web spider (*Atrax robustus*) is a threat to life only in the Sydney region. It is black and big – up to 7 cm across between leg-tips. Treat a funnel-web bite like a snakebite, with pressure bandaging and immobilisation. One other dangerous spider, the redback, may be found anywhere in Australia. Dark, with an orange-red stripe on its back, and measuring 2-3 cm across, its venom is slower-acting and bandaging is unnecessary if medical aid can be obtained quickly.

Bush ticks abound in eastern forests. Tiny when they attach themselves, they burrow into the skin and feed on blood for three or four days, swelling to about 1 cm across. Meanwhile they release a paralysing toxin that can lead to death, especially in children. If you have brushed through dense vegetation, inspect exposed areas of skin for the next three days – and have someone else examine your scalp. A lightly attached tick may be scraped off. One

Rangers and police practise rescue techniques in the Labyrinth at Cradle Mountain-Lake St Clair, Tas

BURNING WITH A PURPOSE

TASMANIAN rangers (pictured below) in Southwest National Park are lighting their own bushfire. It will turn hundreds of hectares into a blackened waste. But these men are making sure that a worse fire will not happen by accident.

The disaster potential of bushfires depends largely on how much fuel they can find. Preventive burning in national parks is ordered before the build-up of litter and undergrowth reaches a dangerous level. Not only the quantity of fuel but also its composition, distribution and moisture content are calculated – in some places with computers.

Frequent burning around the edges of parks is normally done by hand, but bigger tracts inside are more often fired with airdropped incendiary capsules. Under most fire management programmes, only small sections of each park have to be burnt and closed off for regeneration. In the southeast, for example, preventive burning of as little as 5 per cent each year is enough to keep a whole area safe from full-scale destruction.

embedded more deeply can be killed with kerosene or turpentine, and perhaps prised out with tweezers. If this is not wholly successful, seek medical help. Leeches, which are bigger and less likely to escape notice in the first place, are seldom harmful. They drop out after about five minutes of feeding, or if killed with a burning cigarette end or twig. Don't pull them out – parts left in may cause an infection.

Big, aggressive saltwater crocodiles are increasing in some tropical parks. Remember, they are just as much at home in fresh water. Observe signs warning against swimming and take special care walking on riverbanks. If you find yourself near a basking crocodile, back off

quietly. Never place yourself in its path to the water. It may use its tail to knock you out of the way – and one blow from a fullgrown 'saltie' could kill you.

Safety first Unless you are a fit and fully experienced bushwalker, stick to established paths and trails. Don't attempt a long journey through rugged or untracked country unless you have a party of at least three – then if someone is in trouble, another can stand by while the third goes for help. Always carry more water than you believe you will need, along with a first-aid kit and a compass, whistle, knife and waterproof matches. Don't start without obtaining up-to-date maps and telling a ranger of your intentions. And don't fail to report back when the trip is over, if you are asked to. Your negligence could spark a wasteful search operation.

If you are lost, assess your food and water supplies and ration them. Don't waste energy by moving about aimlessly. Seek shelter near an open space where signals can be seen from aircraft, and stay put. If you are forced to keep moving, leave messages along your route or mark it in some way, indicating your direction. To attract attention if other people seem to be nearby, give three whistles, shouts or mirror-flashes at regular intervals, and light a smoky fire of leaves or grass.

Fire-watching from the summit of Mt Lofty becomes a fulltime job during danger periods at Cleland Conservation Park, near Adelaide. Below: Backburning to contain a fast-moving wildfire

How the public can help

IF YOU WOULD enjoy using some spare time to help maintain and improve a favourite national park, just ask. Almost certainly you will be put in touch with a band of volunteers already in action in the district. Most parks – especially those near major population centres – have arrangements with outside groups.

Hundreds of Australians find agreeable fresh-air exercise in voluntary park work at weekends and during holidays. There is room for more. Many tasks are menial: litter removal, weeding and tree planting are typical. But other jobs are highly constructive and add significantly to park amenities. Some are funded by community service clubs and business organisations.

Rapid volunteer response is credited with saving major parts of parks threatened by severe erosion after storm damage. Others, devastated by fire or flooding, have been brought back into public use surprisingly quickly thanks to donated labour. Sometimes a task is long overdue, but simply too hard for the park service to justify on a limited budget. 'Friends of the Prom', for example, trekked back and forth between Melbourne and Wilsons Promontory National Park to remove decades of painted graffiti from rocks at Refuge Cove.

Volunteers with manual trade skills, or experience in plant care on a large scale, are usually most welcome. Others who are adept at dealing with visitors, and can acquire the knowledge to interpret a park's natural fea-

Queensland volunteers pitch in to clear a trail

tures and answer questions, may be enlisted at busy times to help at information centres or take parties on guided walks.

The Australian Trust for Conservation Volunteers, originating in Victoria but spreading nationwide in 1984, offers mobile squads of young people for national park assignments. These task forces usually camp on the site. Their first big accomplishment, in 1982, was the construction of 4.5 km of rabbit fencing at Hattah-Kulkyne National Park. Since then they have restored jetties, improved tracks, built footbridges and eradicated noxious weeds at various parks – and even cleaned up a disused guesthouse to accommodate visitors.

Members of the public are also entitled to have their say in the planning of national parks – where they should be and what activities

should be allowed in them. Management plans are published, and in some states and the ACT the law demands that public comment be invited. Even without such a provision, there is nothing to stop an interested citizen making representations to the appropriate parks service or environment department. A sympathetic MP would probably give assistance.

But individuals have a hard time making themselves heard on national parks issues. Most arguments are too technical, resting on resource evaluations and environmental impact assessments. People seeking to sway government or park management decisions are advised to consult one of the National Parks Associations or a similar organisation.

ORGANISATIONS YOU CAN JOIN

PUBLIC organisations in every state and territory work for the establishment of new national parks, and generally to see that natural environments are not only conserved but also enjoyed.

National Parks Associations, which advance detailed cases to governments for the creation of new parks, are based in Sydney, Melbourne, Brisbane and Canberra. Equivalent bodies elsewhere are the SA Nature Conservation Society (Adelaide), the WA Conservation Council (Perth), the Tasmanian Conservation Trust (Hobart) and the NT Environment Council (Darwin).

National Parks and Wildlife Foundations, which conduct fund-raising appeals – such as NSW's annual 'Operation Noah' – to help acquire land for parks and conserve endangered animals, are based in Sydney and Adelaide. The **Australian Conservation Foundation,** with headquarters in Melbourne, focuses attention on wider environmental issues at a national level, but gives particular support to the national parks movement.

National Trusts, besides their work to save items of cultural heritage such as historic buildings, are active in promoting nature conservation. They have offices in all capital cities. The **Wilderness Society,** having triumphed in its No Dams campaign in Tasmania, has set up branches in nearly all mainland capitals.

World Wildlife Fund Australia, based in Sydney, raises money to preserve endangered species in Australia and some nearby Pacific islands. **Environment Centres** in all capitals and in many provincial cities provide public information and administrative facilities for the environmental movement as a whole. They can give you details of hundreds of other local and special-interest groups that may suit your purpose.

NOTE: Addresses at back of book

Outside helpers remove thorn apple, a noxious weed, from a creekbed in Snowy River National Park, Vic

Making the most of your visit

CREATION of a national park is no guarantee of stunning scenery or exciting activities. Australia's 500-odd parks are meant to preserve widely different environments. Not all may be to your liking. Many will lack the facilities to meet your particular needs. So in planning a visit, make sure you know what to expect.

From information in the regional guide sections that follow, readers can decide for themselves which parks are likely to hold most attraction and how much time they want to spend in them. Descriptions are down to earth – not glamorised. And the interest ratings are equally realistic. If a park rates low in 'day activities', for example, it means there is little to do but look around. There may not be enough to keep children amused for long.

In arranging a tourist itinerary, check on the availability of campsites. If you are interested in visiting several parks it may not be necessary to contact them all in advance – the capital city head office of the National Parks Service should be able to warn you of any difficulty. Queensland has a tourist pre-booking system, operated from Brisbane and regional offices, that covers all of its camping parks.

Consider the time of year and the weather, especially if a long journey outside your home district is involved. Most parks in the tropics, and many others inland, are far from enjoyable in summer. In the bushfire season, or if there have been heavy rains, call the enquiries number before setting out, to make sure that the park of your choice is open and accessible.

If you are travelling with a dog or cat, remember that you cannot take it into a national park. The menace that an escaped cat presents to wildlife is obvious. Few dogs are such efficient hunters – but their mere barking is enough to terrify native animals and disrupt their living patterns for days afterwards.

When you arrive at a park, or at a town office that looks after camping permits, pick up all the explanatory material offered. Anything that heightens your powers of observation will increase your enjoyment. And without full information, you may miss major points of interest. Nearly all parks have general maps. Some have leaflets to aid in bird spotting and plant identification, and special maps for bushwalks and self-guiding nature trails.

Public roads are kept to a minimum in all parks. Be prepared to leave your car in a designated parking area – never drive it into the bush – and see the sights on foot. It is by far the best way. Leaflets or signposts will tell you how long a walk should take, and whether it presents any difficulty.

Knowledge adds interest: an excellent example of park literature from the Northern Territory

NATURE'S BOARDING HOUSE

CONSERVATION COMMISSION NORTHERN TERRITORY

The laziest boarders of them all may be the **aphids**. They stick their needle-like mouths into the sapstream of young leaves and the tree pumps them full of food.

Tree pressure forces sap to ooze from **aphids**' bodies so they become live drinking straws for ants who rush to drink the sweet syrup.

The boarding house can also be a home for invalids, such as the plants-without-roots we call **mistletoes**. In its leaves, each mistletoe makes its own food, but to do this it must use water and minerals gathered by the roots of the tree on which it lives.

When a termite-eaten tree branch snaps off, the front door of a home for **parrots, owls, bats** and many smaller animals is opened. Did you know that nearly one in every five of Australia's different birds depends on such nesting hollows?

Being a night hunter, the flat **Huntsman spider** is grateful to squeeze under the tree's loose bark and spend the daylight hours hidden from hungry birds.

In the six colder months, this River Red Gum showers the ground with millions of tiny seeds. To **ants**, these scattered seeds add up to a huge harvest of food which is eagerly gathered and stored in their underground silos.

From their dark basement home, **termite** carpenters constantly eat through the tree's dead inner wood carving out new rooms for other guests.

The special housing needs of nesting **birds** include a leafy roof to shade and hide their young so they don't become an easy meal for sharp-eyed hawks.

To bush creatures, **flowers** signal 'food'. The parrots arrive early to eat unopened flowerbuds and return later with the bees, ants and other birds to feast on the flowers' nectar and pollen.

Like a horde of teenagers, the tree's **caterpillar** boarders eat all the time to feed bodies that are fast becoming adult. Luckily for the tree, they are gone in a month or two when each caterpillar has become a butterfly, moth or beetle.

Inside this bottle is the most important thing any tree gives to its boarders – **oxygen**. Running silently for years and using only the power of the sun, these marvellous air-conditioners continually replace the oxygen used by all animals.

Tunnelling through a mine of food, unseen **borer** grubs eat for months in the tree's woody sapstream until they leave as adult beetles or moths.

In the hollows of fallen branches **lizards** find snug quarters for winter hibernation and in summer, they're a great place to cool off or quickly escape from hawks.

Living on the ground floor, bush **cockroaches** are night workers using the fallen leaves as their daytime resting place.

RIVER RED GUMS, CENTRAL AUSTRALIA.

...OURS TO PROTECT.

Trees are important. They provide homes, food and shelter for animals, including man, and act as air-conditioners, replacing the oxygen used by every thing that breathes.

Throughout the world trees are rapidly disappearing to make space for farms and towns and to be harvested for timber and products such as paper.

Support the 3 r's of tree conservation by: **retaining** trees; **replanting** trees; and **reducing** your use of tree products to a level our forests can continue to support.

On the back of this poster are other ways you can get to know trees better.

The numbat, a rare termite eater, is protected at Dryandra Forest, WA

Scientists are intrigued by Eungella's gastric-brooding frog

Where animals

WERRIKIMBE National Park gained an extra 20 000 hectares of rainforest in 1984 – all for the sake of some mice. They are of a native species found in significant numbers only two years before. Now their home, on the upper Hastings River in northern NSW, should be secure.

Queensland has dedicated one of its national parks solely to preserve the habitat of an endangered species. The northern hairy-nosed wombat survives only at Epping Forest – formerly part of a cattle station on flat, semi-arid woodland west of Gladstone. Fencing keeps out grazing livestock and allows the regeneration of native grasses and scrub on which the wombat colony depends.

Successful husbandry of rare animals – especially those newly discovered – relies on complicated biological research and the scientific monitoring of populations and feeding habits. Only the national parks and wildlife services have the specialised resources for such work, so most conservation efforts are centred on their parks, or on some state parks under their management. Forestry and water catchment authorities play important co-operative roles.

A recent triumph of wildlife conservation has been the saving of the malleefowl in Victoria. It is the world's only mound-nesting bird living in arid regions. Clearing and grazing of its scrub habitats, along with bushfires, had all but wiped it out by the 1950s. But populations flourish

Parks were specially dedicated to rescue the endangered malleefowl. The male spends 8 months every year building a mound in which eggs are buried

Right: Only Kakadu, NT, has Leichhardt's grasshopper

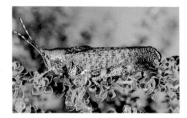

For half a century the Hastings River mouse was known only from English museum specimens. Now it has a park section all to itself, where researchers are trying to discover its habits

Iron Range, Qld, is a haven for the golden-shouldered parrot

Left: A Queensland ranger examines a ghost bat – our only carnivorous species. Big colonies are seen at Fitzroy Caves and nearby Mt Etna

find safety

now in Little Desert, Hattah-Kulkyne and Wyperfeld National Parks. Mallee Cliffs National Park, in far western NSW, was established with the same aim.

Judging whether a species is truly rare can be difficult in Australia. Much of the fauna is small, secretive and nocturnal in habit. It is hard to find, let alone to count. And fires, floods and prolonged droughts lead to drastic fluctuations in numbers and distribution.

A highly unusual frog, discovered in 1972, disappeared after 1979. It lived in Kondalilla National Park and the neighbouring Conondale and Blackall Ranges of south-eastern Queensland. Called the platypus frog because of its swimming action, it seemed to be the only frog in the world that never left water. And it was the world's only known gastric-brooding vertebrate. Females swallowed fertilised eggs and raised their young in their stomachs – somehow shutting off the production of digestive acids.

Rediscovery was hailed in 1983, when similar orange-coloured gastric-brooders were spotted far to the north in Finch Hatton Gorge, which leads out of Eungella National Park. But a captured specimen, compared with one of the Kondalilla frogs still alive in an Adelaide laboratory, proved to belong to yet another new species. The likelihood of other finds offers medical researchers high hopes of developing a drug to prevent human stomach ulcers.

The task of tallying animal populations is full of such surprises. Camping out in 1982 to count waterfowl, a wildlife officer in northwestern Tasmania made a convincing observation of a thylacine, or marsupial 'tiger'. Most people thought the species was extinct. But this animal's doglike head and black-striped, tawny back were unmistakable. Word of the sighting was withheld from the public for two years. If the breeding grounds of thylacines are traced, they will receive the strictest protection ever known.

Skunk-like in its markings, the striped possum of tropical rainforest parks is also remarkably smelly

Nature gets another chance

WOUNDED LANDSCAPES are hard to heal. Even where full restoration is possible, the cost is often prohibitive. But national parks staff are succeeding, here and there, in turning back the clock. Their techniques were largely developed in old-established parks degraded by decades of heavy visiting. Now they are applied to recently re-sumed land that has suffered from other uses.

Most new inland parks have been at least partly grazed by livestock. The effect on natural vegetation is compounded by the persistence of feral animals – species that were introduced as domestic stock but now breed in the wild. Goats and pigs do the most widespread damage. Wild rabbits still bare the land in some districts, in spite of the sweeping eradication measures of the 1950s. High-country parks are often scarred by old logging trails or forestry roads, their margins invaded by exotic weeds. Steeper slopes may be subject to soil erosion.

When coastal parks are acquired, they frequently come with a legacy of dune erosion from off-road vehicles and ill-placed walking tracks. Many include old sand mining leases, or quarries where lime or building stone were extracted. Before the usual chores of removing noxious weeds and planting sand-binding grasses can start, the original land contours may have to be rebuilt.

Some park areas have a history of military use. They were taken over still bearing the marks of bombing or artillery practice and infantry exercises. Among the latest acquisitions are the various high headlands that make up most of Sydney Harbour National Park. These would not be available to the public now – suburban housing would have enveloped them – if they had not been reserved for 150 years or more as defence posts. Vantage points are capped with gun emplacements; the sandstone below is riddled with ammunition chambers, snipers' slits and connecting tunnels. The fortifications are worth keeping for their historical value – but their bare surroundings, stripped of soil by wind erosion, were an eyesore. Years of work and substantial funds are going into restoration

Sand mining roads scar a proposed park extension on Nth Stradbroke Island, Qld

Right: Regeneration of grazed land on Bogong High Plains, Vic, is a co-operative venture

MELBOURNE UNIVERSITY BOTANY SCH
SOIL CONSERVATION AUTHORITY
STATE ELECTRICITY COMMISSION

EXPERIMENTAL PLOTS

PLEASE WALK OUTSIDE THE PLOTS
'TRAMPLING' DAMAGES THE VEGETAT

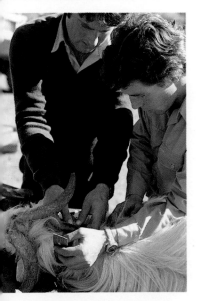

A goat is fitted with a radio collar to track its movements

of the heaths and woodlands that greeted the First Fleet.

Bush regeneration calls for fine judgment, skilled work and inexhaustible patience. Attempts to make dramatic improvements overnight, simply by ripping out alien weeds or dumping new topsoil, are bound to fail. The same weeds – if not worse ones that are even faster-growing – will reappear, and probably work their way deeper into any natural bush nearby. Only a cautious approach, aimed at tipping the balance subtly towards native plants, is likely to succeed.

Managed regeneration of weed-infested bush starts from the least affected area and works towards the most degraded. In weeding, the soil is disturbed as little as possible and surface mulch is put back in place so that any native seeds lie at the proper level. The pace of progress is dictated by the capacity of seedlings to re-claim territory. They must have time to form a dense, diverse community in one zone – and planners must be convinced that it can be kept clear of weeds – before a neighbouring area is touched.

In rainforests the process is complicated by the inter-action of plants. The different growth habits of weeds have to be considered, so that they are taken out in the correct order. If tall, leafy vines are removed first, for example, stronger light reaching the forest floor may spur the spread of ground creepers that choke off native seed-ling growth. Extensive regeneration projects, whether of rainforest trees or of eucalypts and their companions, take many years.

Control of feral animals calls for just as much patience. Little is achieved without a thorough knowledge of how they live in particular habitats. The breeding rate of a species may vary from place to place, depending mainly on climate and the availability of food. Patterns of move-ment also vary. Some plants and land are more easily damaged than others. All these factors influence a deci-sion on how much control – which usually means killing – is necessary in a park, and what method will work best.

Wildlife suffers heavily from predation by feral cats and dogs and dingoes, and from the competition these and other species create for food, water and shelter. Rabbits and goats strip any vegetation they can reach

THE SCOURGE OF NATIVE WILDLIFE

CATS breeding in the wild are the most efficient of all predators. Their chief impact is on native birds, small mammals and reptiles. Indirectly they can also upset plant life, because they eat many of the animals that control insect pests.

Nearly all feral cats revert to a tabby appearance. Most are greyish, but on red outback soils more are ginger. In forested regions, where food is easily obtained, they are heavier than domestic cats but not noticeably bigger.

But in harsher country, it is survival of the fittest. The most powerful cats get the food – and the biggest toms take all the breeding opportunities. Supercats are evolving. Some stand twice as tall as their ancestors and are many times heavier. One giant shot in the Simpson Desert weighed 12 kg.

above ground, and pigs do even worse – they root into the soil with their snouts and leave it fit for nothing but weeds. Water buffalo in the Northern Territory trample and degrade wetlands that are important to tourism and vital to migratory waterfowl. And many feral species are potential carriers of exotic livestock diseases – tubercu-losis and brucellosis, for example – that in uncontrolled conditions could be ruinous to the agricultural economy. In their extermination measures, parks services work in close co-operation with farming communities.

Feral pigs lay waste a waterhole at Kinchega, NSW

Trees return to former farmland at Organ Pipes, Vic

Mt Lidgbird on Lord Howe Island rises 777 metres from the edge of a coral-encrusted lagoon. The Lord Howe group, 700 km northeast of Sydney, is regarded as an outstanding example of an island system developed from submarine volcanic activity. Many of its plants and animals are found nowhere else. Much of the main island is protected under NSW national parks and wildlife laws as a 'permanent park'

Below: Forests crowd the deep gorge of the Franklin River in Wild Rivers National Park. This park forms the centre of the western Tasmanian World Heritage area, together with the neighbouring Southwest and Cradle Mountain-Lake St Clair National Parks

An obligation

NATURAL FEATURES of Australia figure importantly as World Heritage sites. Already listed are the Great Barrier Reef, Kakadu National Park, western Tasmania's chain of wilderness parks, the Willandra Lakes region of NSW, the Lord Howe Island group, and the rainforest parks and reserves of northern NSW. Uluru National Park, embracing Ayers Rock, is expected to be added.

Some great national parks overseas, such as Grand Canyon and Yellowstone in the USA, are among the nearly 200 other 'properties' on the list. But the majority are sites of ancient civilisations, or manmade structures of cultural importance. They include many famous cathedrals and palaces — along with the infamous Auschwitz concentration camp.

Inclusion of a natural area is a source of pride to any country. It confers recognition that the area is of world significance because it: represents a major stage of the

THE ANCIENT ROCK ART OF KAKADU

ABORIGINAL sites in Kakadu National Park, occupied for at least 25 000 years, include rock galleries of elaborate prehistoric paintings. Pictured are two from the hundreds seen by visitors to Ubirr (Obiri Rock).

to the world

Sand lunettes, windblown from the beds of the dried-up Willandra Lakes, hold evidence of human activity more than 30 000 years ago

earth's evolution; exemplifies continuing geological processes, biological evolution and human interaction with the environment; contains rare or superlative natural features or areas of exceptional beauty; or supports rare or endangered plants and animals.

But along with pride goes a heavy obligation. When a site is nominated for World Heritage listing, the nation responsible undertakes to ensure 'identification, protection, conservation, presentation and transmission to future generations ... to the utmost of its own resources'. The nominating nation is also obliged to obtain international assistance if it is needed to achieve those aims.

Some loss of sovereignty and secrecy is implied. That may be why the world list is noticeably incomplete: some countries refuse to compromise their privacy. In Australia's case the commitment made by the federal government clearly overrides states' rights. That was established

The Great Barrier Reef is the biggest Heritage area of all

in the High Court over the Tasmanian dam argument.

Australia's nominations are proposed by the Australian Heritage Commission. Its chairman and six members are part-timers appointed by the federal Environment Minister and drawn from a variety of professions in all states. They also supervise the selection and documentation of other important natural or cultural sites in Australia, and the compilation of a register of what is called the National Estate. Fraser Island, when it was rescued from sand mining, became the inaugural entry on that local list.

World Heritage nominations are received at UNESCO headquarters in Paris. Seventy countries have signed the convention that governs the listing procedure. Nominations go before a committee of 21 national representatives, with a membership that changes frequently so that every country gets a turn. The committee meets to approve listings towards the end of each year.

PART THREE

A guide to the national parks of Queensland

Parks are grouped on the basis of their accessibility from major population centres and their proximity to one another. In each region a pictorial selection is followed by a directory of parks. It gives their location, indicates their character and identifies the public facilities they offer. Comparative ratings, assessed by parks staff, are aimed at helping visitors decide on the destinations that will give them most satisfaction. As a further aid, the activities allowed in national parks are listed along with the parks in which they may be pursued.

BRISBANE REGION

The finest park stays on the drawing-board

OVERWHELMING in their numbers, the national parks of southeastern Queensland are sadly fragmented. Tamborine Mountain alone has no fewer than eight parks – scattered, heavily used and so tiny that their bushland could not sustain itself without intensive management. They are enchanting as picnic grounds, but by any national or international standard they do not deserve their titles.

Residential and horticultural development has advanced too far at Tamborine to allow much hope of amalgamating pocket-handkerchief parks into more naturally viable units. In many other areas agricultural clearance or forestry logging have left small parks isolated and incapable of expansion. But one chance remains to make the Brisbane region the focus of worldwide admiration among conservationists. So close to a major city, a Scenic Rim National Park would have no match.

Scarps and peaks of the Great Divide form a band of broken, forested high country from Mt Mistake, near Toowoomba, to the NSW border. There the McPherson Range veers east as a rampart of the Tweed volcanic basin and runs almost to the coast near Coolangatta. Nearly all of this splendid arc, spanning more than 300 km, is wilderness.

Proposals to link existing national parks of the Scenic Rim have been mooted in Brisbane for at least 40 years. In 1980 there were 20 parks. Enlargements and amalgamations at Main Range and Mt Barney have cut the tally to 15. Apart from some other areas with the lower status of environmental parks, most of the remainder is under state forestry department control. Parks and forestry officials confer on policies and an overall management plan is being developed. Amalgamation of all these reserves into one park, if legislators should see fit, seems only a short further step to take.

If the political vision and resolve were found, an even grander dream could be realised. The Queensland-New South Wales border, drawn along the McPherson Range and the northern rim of the Tweed basin, divides a region of natural integrity. Landforms and plant and animal groups make up two halves of the one geographical unit. Border Ranges National Park, controlled from Sydney, is simply a continuation of Lamington. Along with the nearby Mt Warning and Nightcap National Parks and a cluster of nature reserves, it forms one of the key areas of unspoiled NSW rainforest, nominated in 1986 for World Heritage listing.

An opportunity exists here to embrace a total environment of highland forests, streams and wildlife habitats in one natural belt, enhancing their chances of survival. At park management level there is already a high degree of co-operation between the states. Needed next are integrated travel routes and a joint publicity programme. Overlooking the country's busiest holiday coast, a continuous two-state park would offer immense benefits to tourism. Seen as a whole, it could rank as the greatest Australian park of all.

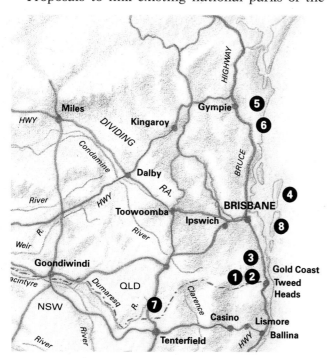

Your access and facilities guide to national parks in this region starts on page 66

Cedar Creek Falls in Tamborine Mountain National Parks

Rock orchids (above) do no harm to host trees, but strangler figs with their twining prop roots (right) can kill. The figs grow from seeds lodged high in other trees – blown there or carried by birds

LAMINGTON NATIONAL PARK

Lord Lamington, governor of Queensland from 1896 to 1902, visited the plateau named in his honour only once – and marked the event by shooting a koala. 'Its cries were terrible,' he was reported as saying 40 years later. Some 100 km south of Brisbane, the state's most popular park, declared in 1915 and now covering more than 20 000 ha, occupies the north-western rim and rivers dissected outer slopes of the ancient Tweed volcano.

The main access roads reach privately run holiday lodges at Binna Burra and Green Mountains. Park picnic and camping grounds adjoin Green Mountain. Walking tracks, ranging in length from 2 km to 24 km, make up a network totalling more than 160 km. Binna Burra has a short 'senses trail' with a guiding rope and Braille de-scriptions. Sighted people are invited to try it blind-folded. Other walks lead through varied forests to look-outs, caves, river gorges and dozens of waterfalls.

Subtropical rainforests including tall red 'cedar' and hoop pine cover most of Lamington. But above 900 metres on the McPherson Range it has the northermost stands of antarctic beech, a temperate rainforest species. There are also areas of wet eucalypt forest, and even some dry heaths surrounded by mallee eucalypts. Bird species include the spine-tailed logrunner, Australian ground thrush, Albert lyrebird and rare rufous scrub bird.

Guinea flower

*Flower-like fungi help to break
down leaf litter (below)*

*Left: Coomera Falls, 5 km south
of Binna Burra, drop 64 metres*

Blechnum, a water fern

Constantly plunging water has worn a hole in the cave roof

Subtropical rainforest spreads a dense canopy over Cave Creek, a Nerang River tributary

Right: Fronds of staghorn Platycerium grande *may grow to nearly 2 metres*

SPRINGBROOK NATIONAL PARK

Waters of Cave Creek, in the Natural Bridge section, plunge through the eroded roof of a basalt cave and flow out through a wide opening that forms a near-perfect arch. It is big enough for groups to enter — though the cave floor is slippery. After dark, the inner recesses are lit by thousands of glow worms in the rock.

This section of the park occupies just over 200 ha of the Numinbah Valley, which descends from the western edge of the Springbrook Plateau and holds the head-waters of the Nerang River. A circuit walk of about 1 km descends from a picnic ground to the creek and cave, returning with a climb over the archway. Subtropical rainforest shrubs and trees crowd the creek.

Another walk of similar distance, but steeper, climbs through cool-temperate rainforest dominated by negro-head beech. It leads to a lookout giving good views of Mt Warning and the craggy rim that remains from the flanks of the Tweed volcano.

The lush, subtropical rainforest does not immediately disclose the cave and bridge for which the area has become famous

TAMBORINE NATIONAL PARK

'Unfit for any other purpose' according to forestry officials, the 130 ha of Witches Falls were proclaimed in 1908 as Queensland's first national park. Seven other areas on the northern slopes of Mt Tamborine have been added to form a disjointed group of parks protecting lookout points, waterfalls and a variety of unspoilt bushland that is surprising in view of their tiny size and heavy use by picnic parties.

Cedar Creek has waterfalls and swimming holes surrounded by eucalypt forests. Joalah and Witches Falls have short walking tracks through the district's best examples of subtropical rainforest. Palm Grove is named for its extensive stand of piccabeen palms, and Macrozamia (or Zamia) Grove for the cycads that abound in its little patch of rainforest and eucalypts.

Buttress roots support a cluster of tall fig trees in MacDonald Park

Piccabeens of Palm Grove are framed in a huge archway formed by the roots of a rainforest tree

*Clumps of moisture-loving vegetation cling to the basalt faces
of Cameron Falls, in the Knoll section*

TAMBORINE
NATIONAL
PARK

*Left: Cedar Creek Falls, in the northernmost part of
Tamborine Park, spill into a chain of good swimming holes.
Above: In Joalah section, higher on the mountainside,
the same creek descends through well-developed
subtropical rainforest*

Curtis Falls are the best-known of many in Joalah. Consistently high rainfall in the Darlington Range, backing the Gold Coast, keeps streams flowing year-round

55

Spitfire Creek spreads into reed-choked marshes on its course between Jabiru Lake and the northeastern coast

MORETON ISLAND NATIONAL PARK

South of a small rock outcrop at Cape Moreton, an island of nearly 19000 ha is built entirely of sand. Low plains, lakes, swamps and windblown dunes surround forested Mt Tempest – at 285 metres the highest stabilised coastal dune in the world. A surf beach runs virtually unbroken for more than 30 km along the eastern shore. The more sheltered west coast has boat anchorages, three small settlements and a resort at Tangalooma – until 1962 the site of Queensland's only whaling station. Inland, except where there are moving dunes and 'blows', the island has sedge and heath communities, melaleuca woodlands and eucalypt forests. Motoring is possible only with four-wheel-drive, and restricted to a few designated tracks. These link the island's three camping grounds.

In March 1986, the then Mount Tempest National Park was expanded to about 15400 ha (89 per cent of the island) and its name changed to **Moreton Island National Park.** The whole of Moreton Island was declared a recreation area in 1991. The area includes the national park and other government lands. A vehicle permit is required as is also a camping permit, and both may be obtained from the barge operators.

Jabiru Lake, its bed cemented by plant and mineral compounds, is perched well above sea level

Below: Tidal pools are trapped among foredunes on the island's northwestern coast

Mt Tempest caps the high dune ridge beyond Blue Lagoon

MORETON ISLAND

A creek fed from Moreton Island's raised water table trickles through the southern 'Little Desert', supporting a sparse growth of grasses

Acids from decaying plant matter stain a creek flowing out to the northwest coast. Volcanic plugs of the Glass House Mountains rise on the skyline, beyond the mainland shore

Cooloola (Great Sandy National Park)

Cooloola presents two faces – one seen by water, another by road. Coastal areas, accessible by 4WD from Rainbow Beach or Noosa, are notable for high dune formations, wind-driven 'blows', multi-coloured sandcliffs and spring-flowering heaths. Campers make for Double Island Point or the outlet of Freshwater Creek, in the north-east of the 39 000 ha park. There is conventional vehicle access to Freshwater by an inland road; a walking track circles the lake.

The gravelled Cooloola Way takes visitors to the Noosa Plain. A 46 km wilderness trail beginning at Mt Mullen, off Rainbow Beach, and ending at Elanda, leads into the forested hills, heathlands and swamps that surround the upper Noosa River. Near an information centre at the head of Lake Cootharaba, a self-guiding nature trail has a boardwalk over mangroves and a hide for observing waterfowl. A 10 km track between Fig Tree Point and Harry Spring's Hut, through vine forest and eucalypt woodlands, takes 2 hours each way. The Noosa is navigable by motor boats to the junction of Teewah Creek; canoeists can go on to the headwaters.

Sedges, mangroves and casuarinas fringe Lake Cootharaba, where sailing is popular but the water is often rough

Flowering spikes of grass-trees stud sandy heathlands beside the Noosa River, reaching to densely wooded dune ridges near the sea. Cooloola's coastal zone is an accumulated mass of transported sand, added to an older mainland by the same ocean forces that built Fraser, Moreton and the Stradbroke Islands

Native hibiscus (above) and melastoma (left) flourish on Cooloola's swampy flats and moist coastal heathlands. Melastoma has sweet, edible fruits

Climbing guinea flower (left) and crinum, a swamp lily, brighten Noosa's coastal heathlands

Noosa National Park

Forested ridges and swampy heathlands behind Noosa Head are preserved in a popular park of 450 ha, wedged between the busy resorts of Noosa Heads and Sunshine Beach. Walking tracks wind around and up Noosa Hill (147 metres). They take in hoop pine rainforest, eucalypt forest, scrubs and flowering heaths. A linking track follows the coastline for 3 km. Laguna Lookout, high in the southwestern corner of the park, has its own access from the Noosa-Cooroy road and requires no walking.

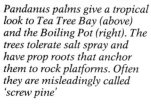

Pandanus palms give a tropical look to Tea Tree Bay (above) and the Boiling Pot (right). The trees tolerate salt spray and have prop roots that anchor them to rock platforms. Often they are misleadingly called 'screw pine'

Left: Fringed lily

GIRRAWEEN NATIONAL PARK

Sharp winter frosts, unusual in most of Queensland, hasten the process of granite weathering that gives Girraween its eye-catching array of outcrops and piled tors – some so finely balanced that they seem to defy gravity. Beyond its purely visual qualities, the 11 000 ha park is of considerable biological interest. It occupies an arm of the New England Tablelands of NSW, and its plant communities are more closely allied with those of the cool south than with any others in Queensland. Eucalypt forests on well-drained slopes and valley floors include Wallangarra whitegum, limited to this district. Swamp communities are common where granite outcrops impede drainage. The scree slopes hold enough soil to form natural rock gardens of flowering heaths and shrubs. Even on the rounded summits, capped by Mt Norman at 1267 metres, lilies and shrubs find an anchorage in rock joints.

Walking tracks radiate from the park headquarters and its two nearby camping grounds. Among the easiest and most interesting is the Granite Arch track, which takes little more than half an hour return. Other routes take 2-4 hours. Mt Norman is a 3 hour walk from the headquarters area but can be approached more easily from a vehicle track passing through the eastern part of the park.

Wattles bloom (left) on the rocky slopes of the Pyramids – high tors in the northern part of Girraween. The park is strewn with huge boulders (above, Balancing Rock at the Pyramids; right, Granite Arch). These result from weathering, mainly by water, of blocks of cracked granite. The original mass formed about 220 million years ago under older sandstones and volcanic formations – long since eroded away

South-easterly currents push a constant procession of waves on to Main Beach, which makes a straight sweep of 35 km from Point Lookout. Heaths and swamps cover a lowland strip between eroding foredunes and wooded hind dunes

BLUE LAKE NATIONAL PARK

North Stradbroke Island is one of three major sand islands separating the waters of Moreton Bay from the Pacific Ocean. It features numerous extensive water areas, including Blue Lake National Park, a quiet haven away from the bustle of the mainland. The park of 501 ha, already damaged by heavy visiting, looked likely to come under disastrous pressure from a rapid increase in sightseers, and conservationists urged the Queensland government to declare a greatly enlarged park. In the early 1990s there were advanced plans to increase the area to cover 50 to 60 per cent of the island.

In the present park, eucalypt woodlands surround the sandy margins of a freshwater 'window' lake, where the island's water table emerges. Popular with swimmers, it is a 2.4 km walk from the park entrance.

Water ferns and other aquatic plants spread over and round Lake Kaboora. Its waters are fresh though the surrounding sands are saline

PARKS OF THE BRISBANE REGION

1. Alton National Park

440 km W, 75 km E of St George. Darling Downs, Maranoa weather district. Moonie Highway skirts park boundary.

Apple, ironbark and cypress pine dominate the woodlands of this 558 ha park. Sandplains rise to low ridges covered by heath and hummock grassland scattered with eucalypts and grass-trees. Spring rains bring wildflowers.

NOTE: Permit required for bushcamping. Fees apply.
BEST TIME: Spring.
TEL: (07) 4639 4599.
FAX: (07) 4639 4524.
ADDRESS: PO Box 731, Toowoomba 4350.

Scenic enjoyment ✓
Day activities ✗
Family camping ✗
Hard bushwalking ✗

2. Bendidee National Park

360 km SW, 32 km NE of Goondiwindi. Darling Downs, Maranoa weather district. Car access off Cunningham Highway 59 km W of Inglewood.

Forest species prolific in the adjoining Bendidee State Forest intrude sparsely into the brigalow and belah scrublands of this undeveloped 930 ha park. Tea-tree, wilga and vines grow among acacias and casuarinas in an area of low rainfall. After a good soaking, however, flowering and fruiting plants attract many birds.

NOTE: Permit required for bushcamping. Fees apply.
BEST TIME: Spring, for wildflowers.
TEL: (07) 4661 3710.
FAX: (07) 4661 7001.
ADDRESS: Hermitage & Research Station via Warwick, 4370.

Scenic enjoyment ✓
Day activities ✗
Family camping ✗
Hard bushwalking ✗

3. Blackall Range National Parks

105–110 km N, 16–22 km W of Nambour. South Coast, Curtis and Moreton weather district. Car access to Mapleton Falls off Nambour–Kenilworth road 3 km W of Mapleton; to Kondalilla off Montville–Flaxton road, leave Bruce Highway at Landsborough. Obi Obi Gorge reached on foot from Baroon Pocket road 12 km N of Maleny or from Western Avenue, 1 km S of Montville.

Heavily timbered mountain parks in the Blackall Range, less than an hour's drive from Sunshine Coast beaches, preserve waterfalls and remnant rainforests in a region largely cleared for farming.

Falls on Skenes Creek in **Kondalilla National Park** (208 ha) drop 80 m over a series of cascades into a misty valley of rainforest with piccabeen palms and distinct bunya pines. A formed 4.5 km walking trail loops around a deep pool at the base of Kondalilla Falls before climbing to lookout points with views over the creek and north to ranges around the headwaters of Mary River. The creek hosts a population of Queensland lungfish, an unusual animal sharing many of the characteristics of amphibians; it is a completely protected species.

A strenuous hike along a rocky creek course from Baroon Pocket leads to Obi Obi Gorge. Steep walls, topped with rainforest rich in epiphytic orchids and ferns, pinch the creek and quicken its flow at the Narrows. A 26 ha park surrounds the lesser cascades of **Mapleton Falls** on a tributary to the lower reaches of Obi Obi Creek. Walking trails from picnic grounds wander through eucalypt forest which intermingles with rainforest on moister slopes.

NOTE: No facilities at Obi Obi Gorge.
WARNING: Obi Obi Creek dangerous after heavy rain. Check with Caloundra-Maroochy water board before visiting in case water is being released.
BEST TIME: Spring, autumn.
TEL: (07) 5494 3983.
ADDRESS: 3 Kondalilla Falls Road, Flaxton via Nambour 4560.

Scenic enjoyment ✓✓✓
Day activities ✓✓✓
Family camping ✗
Hard bushwalking ✓

4. Blue Lake National Park

60 km E, 10 km E of Dunwich on North Stradbroke Island. South Coast, Curtis and Moreton weather district. Car access to park boundary from Dunwich. Car ferries to Dunwich from Redland Bay and Cleveland.

DESCRIPTION: Page 64.
NOTE: No camping in park.
BEST TIME: Year-round.
TEL: (07) 3286 9261.
FAX: (07) 3826 6240.
ADDRESS: PO Box 402, Cleveland 4163.

Scenic enjoyment ✓✓
Day activities ✓✓
Family camping ✗
Hard bushwalking ✗

5 Bunya Mountains National Park

240 km NW, 60 km S of Kingaroy. Darling Downs, Wide Bay and Burnett weather districts. Car access off Warrego Highway at Jondaryan or Dalby.

The largest remaining natural stand of bunya pines, a species greatly depleted by early rainforest timber-getters, was preserved in this 11 700 ha park in 1908. It was Queensland's second national park and is one of the state's most popular, with easy access off a sealed through road, big picnic grounds, a kiosk and three camping areas. Walking trails form a network through the dense bunya pine and hoop pine rainforest, leading to waterfalls, gorges and lookouts over the Darling Downs and South Burnett.

Before European settlement of the area Aboriginal tribes gathered here to feast on the plentiful crop of nuts from the bunya pine. The nuts, about the size of a small hen's egg, grow in big cones in the rounded crown of the tree.

NOTE: Fees and permits apply in the park's campgrounds.
BEST TIME: Spring, autumn.
TEL: (07) 4668 3127.
FAX: (07) 4668 3116.
ADDRESS: MS 501, via Dalby 4405.

Scenic enjoyment ✓✓✓
Day activities ✓✓✓
Family camping ✓✓✓
Hard bushwalking ✓✓

6. Burleigh Head National Park

90 km S, 15 km S of Southport. South Coast, Curtis and Moreton weather district. Car access off Pacific Highway at Burleigh Heads or off Gold Coast Highway.

Basalt boulders line the shores below Big Burleigh, a steep headland at the entrance to Tallebudgera Creek hemmed in by intense residential and tourist development along the Gold Coast.

Short nature trails loop through the 28 ha park, sampling vine forest, tall eucalypt forest, low woodland with pandanus and patches of tussock grassland.

BEST TIME: Year-round.
TEL: (07) 5535 3032.
ADDRESS: PO Box 612, Burleigh Heads 4220.

Scenic enjoyment ✓✓
Day activities ✓
Family camping ✗
Hard bushwalking ✗

7. Conondale National Park

140 km NW. South Coast, Curtis and Moreton weather district. Car access to both park sections off Conondale–Kenilworth road. Turn off Bruce Highway at Landsborough.

Tangled woody vines in tall rainforest with flooded gums, bunya pines and palms cover the mountainous slopes of this 2000 ha park. The area is an undeveloped wilderness reserve, without tracks or facilities of any kind. Visitors reach the edges of the park along rough backblock tracks, but rarely attempt the daunting trek into the dense forest undergrowth.

BEST TIME: Spring.
TEL: (07) 5494 3983.
ADDRESS: Park Road, Noosa Heads 4567.

Scenic enjoyment ✓✓
Day activities ✗
Family camping ✗
Hard bushwalking ✗

8. Cooloola (Great Sandy National Park)

230 km N, 65 km NE of Gympie. South Coast, Curtis and Moreton weather district. Northern section accessible from Gympie–Rainbow Beach road or from Noosa (by 4WD) via ferry and along beach. Southern section accessible by boat from Boreen Point, Elanda and Tewantin. Tours operate from Rainbow Beach as well as Noosa and Tewantin.

DESCRIPTION: Page 60. **Noosa River National Park** (469 ha) preserves an undeveloped area of forest and swamp communities on the river's southern banks downstream from Lake Cootharaba. **Mount Pinbarren National Park** (23 ha) covers a peak clothed in hoop pine rainforest in the uplands west of Cooloola, about 5 km north of Pomona. **Pipeclay National Park** (2 ha) preserves an Aboriginal ceremonial site off the Rainbow Beach road. **Mount Coolum National Park** (63 ha), between Maroochydore and Noosa, is a prominent Sunshine coat landmark; a rough track winds to the mountain top where panoramic views can be enjoyed.

Lake Weyba National Park

(1138 ha), southwest of Noosa, preserves the Sunshine Coast's high dunes along with heath and scribbly gum forest; the lake itself is a fish habitat reserve. A stretch of coastal wilderness, 25 km southeast of Maryborough and accessed from the Maryborough–Boonooroo road, was established as **Poona National Park** (4250 ha) in 1990–91 to protect an important example of wallum flora; the area is also rich in birdlife, including the endangered ground parrot.

VISITOR CENTRE: Off Kinaba Island – boat access; walking track from Elanda.
NOTE: Camping requires permit and fees apply.
BEST TIME: Spring, autumn.
TEL: (07) 5449 7364 (southern section); 5485 3245 (northern).
ADDRESS: Elanda Point via Tewantin 4565 (s. Cooloola); PO Box 30, Rainbow Beach 4581 (n. Cooloola).

Scenic enjoyment ✓✓✓
Day activities ✓✓✓
Family camping ✓✓✓
Walking, canoeing ✓

9. Crows Nest National Park

180 km W, 45 km N of Toowoomba. Granite Belt weather district. Car access to northern section along sealed road E from Crows Nest.

Perseverance Creek flows over huge boulders on its course north from the man-made lake of Perseverance Dam. Eucalypt forest and heathland cover high ground and ridges above the creek and the glistening granite gorge of Crows Nest Falls. Tall rainforest thrives in the sheltered environment around deep pools enjoyed by swimmers. Short trails branch off a main walking track from popular picnic grounds. It takes about 2 hours to explore the northern section of this 1020 ha park.

The undeveloped southern section of the park, often referred to as **Perseverance Section,** is southwest of the dam. Walkers find their own way into its forests.

NOTE: Permit required for camping, fees apply.
BEST TIME: Autumn, spring.
TEL: (07) 4698 1296.
ADDRESS: PO Box 68, Crows Nest 4355.

Scenic enjoyment ✓✓
Day activities ✓✓
Family camping ✓✓
Hard bushwalking ✓

10. D'Aguilar Range National Parks

40 km NW. South Coast, Curtis and Moreton weather district. Car access by sealed road via

1 Alton NP

2 Bendidee NP

3 Blackall Range NPs

4 Blue Lake NP

5 Bunya Mountains NP

6 Burleigh Head NP

7 Conondale NP

8 Cooloola NP

9 Crows Nest NP

10 D'Aguilar Range NPs

11 Fort Lytton NP

12 Freshwater Creek NP

13 Girraween NP

14 Glass House Mountains NPs

15 Lamington NP

16 Main Range NP

17 Moogerah Peaks NPs

18 Mooloolah River NP

19 Moreton Island NP

20 Mount Barney NP

21 Mount Mistake NP

22 Noosa NP

23 Sunshine Coast NPs

24 Bribie Island NP

25 Queen Mary Falls NP

26 Ravensbourne NP

27 Rocky Creek NP

28 St Helena Island NP

29 Southwood NP

30 Springbrook NPs

31 Sundown NP

32 Tamborine NP

33 The Palms NP

Waterworks and Mt Nebo Roads.

A steep, narrow road from the outskirts of Brisbane climbs mountain slopes covered in eucalypt forest and rainforest to a string of national parks below the high peaks of D'Aguilar Range.

A walking trail through adjoining state forest links the two smallest parks, **Jolly's Lookout** (11 ha) with its sweeping views over the Samford Valley, and **Boombana** (38 ha); both parks are popular for picnics. A circuit track in Boombana passes some superb examples of red bloodwood and small-leaf fig.

Cabbage tree palms are the most prominent feature of **Manorina National Park** (139 ha) on the trail to Mt Nebo Lookout.

A self-guiding nature walk in **Maiala National Park** (1140 ha) helps visitors identify trees and understand rainforest ecology. Longer walks lead along creek banks to Greene's Falls, and through an impressive rainforest.
NOTE: Camping at Manorina.
BEST TIME: Year-round.
TEL: (07) 3289 0200.
FAX: (07) 3300 5347.
ADDRESS: 60 Mt Nebo Road, The Gap 4060.

Scenic enjoyment ✔✔
Day activities ✔✔✔
Family camping ✔
Hard bushwalking ✔

11. Fort Lytton National Park
16 km NE. South Coast, Curtis and Moreton weather district. Car access via Lytton Road to South Street, Lytton.

The fort, a typical 19th-century garrison, is the principal remaining landmark of a military encampment designed to counter any determined effort by enemy ships to attack the Port of Brisbane. For 40 years, between 1860 and 1900, it was the focus of Queensland's defence activity.
NOTES: Open 10.00–16.00 (not Saturdays); advance bookings may be necessary.
BEST TIME: Year-round.
TEL: (07) 3393 4647.
FAX: (07) 3893 1780.
ADDRESS: PO Box 293, Wynnum 4178.

12. Freshwater Creek (Great Sandy National Park)
35 km N, 15 km NW of Redcliffe. South Coast, Curtis and Moreton weather district. Bruce Highway skirts the park. Part of Cooloola section of Great Sandy NP.

An important remnant of wallum country with banksias, eucalypts and grass-trees is preserved in this park of nearly 100 ha. The area is of mainly scientific interest as a representative sample of a vegetation type fast disappearing from south Queensland.
BEST TIME: Spring, autumn.
TEL, ADDRESS AND FAX: As for Cooloola.

Scenic enjoyment ✔
Day activities ✘
Family camping ✘
Hard bushwalking ✘

13. Girraween National Park
260 km SW, 34 km S of Stanthorpe. Granite Belt weather district. Car access off New England Highway 26 km S of Stanthorpe.
DESCRIPTION: Page 63.
VISITOR CENTRE: Park headquarters.
BEST TIME: Spring.
TEL: (07) 4684 5157.
FAX: (07) 4684 5123.
ADDRESS: Via Ballandean 4382.

Scenic enjoyment ✔✔✔
Day activities ✔✔
Family camping ✔✔✔
Hard bushwalking ✔✔✔

14. Glass House Mountains National Parks
65 km N. South Coast, Curtis and Moreton weather district. Car access off Bruce Highway between Beerburrum and Glass House Mountains township.

Domed hills and lopsided peaks of the Glass House Mountains rise abruptly from low plains behind the Sunshine Coast. The nine tallest hills, as well as several lower prominences, mark the centres of separate volcanic eruptions around 25 million years ago. Eroded remnants of the volcanic plugs are preserved in four national parks. **Beerwah** (245 ha), **Coonowrin** (113 ha), **Ngungun** (49 ha) and **Tibrogargan** (219 ha).

Well-defined but rough and unmaintained tracks have been trodden through each of the parks and, with the exception of Mt Coonowrin, the peaks can be climbed by energetic hikers prepared for some steep clambering over rocks. Mt Coonowrin (375 m) and the east face of Mt Tibrogargan (291 m) should only be attempted by experienced rock climbers.

Rainforest species occur in small pockets of closed forest, but eucalypt forest including ironbark, bloodwood, blackbutt and tallow wood dominates the lower slopes. Heath plants grow in areas of shallow soil on steep rocks. Ground orchids are common.

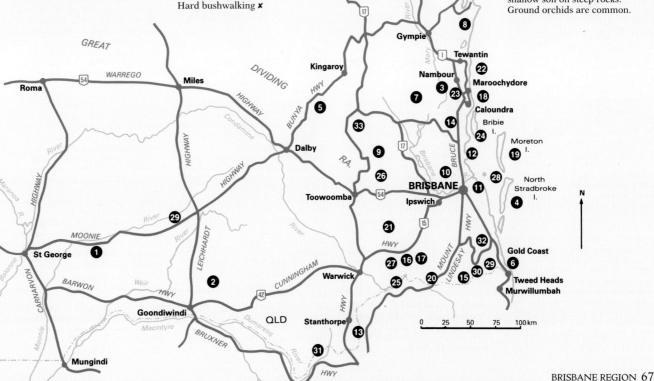

NOTE: Camping is not permitted inside the park.
BEST TIME: Spring, autumn.
TEL: (07) 5494 3983.
ADDRESS: 61 Bunya Street, Naleny 4557.

Scenic enjoyment ✔✔
Day activities ✔
Family camping ✗
Hard bushwalking ✔

15. Lamington National Park

107 km S. South Coast, Curtis and Moreton weather district. Car access S of Pacific Highway from Beenleigh via Canungra, or from Nerang via Beechmont.
DESCRIPTION: Page 48.
Mount Chinghee National Park (722 ha) to the west of Lamington covers undeveloped spurs, ridges and slopes of vine forest with hoop pine emerging above the high canopy. The park is reached on foot from the Lions Tourist Road south of Mt Lindesay Highway at Innisplain. **Sarabah National Park** preserves an almost pure stand of black bean trees covering 1 ha on the road from Canungra to Green Mountains.
NOTE: No bush camping within 4 km of Binna Burra or O'Reilly's lodges. Visitors should 'tread lightly'; there is a real possibility otherwise that bush camping will be further restricted or even prohibited. A helpful leaflet explaining minimal impact camping techniques is available. Permits are required and fees are payable.
BEST TIME: Spring, autumn.
TEL: (07) 5533 3584.
ADDRESS: Via Nerang 4211.

Scenic enjoyment ✔✔✔
Day activities ✔✔
Family camping ✔✔✔
Hard bushwalking ✔✔✔

16. Main Range National Park

115 km SW. South Coast, Curtis and Moreton weather district. Cunningham Highway crosses park. Southern area reached by rough dry-weather track between Boonah and Killarney.

Mt Mitchell and Mt Cordeaux form the steep ridges of Cunningham's Gap, a deep saddle in the Main Range that allows Cunningham Highway to run easily west towards Warwick. Walking tracks from camping and picnic grounds around the highway lead north and south to the mountain peaks through areas of rainforest, grassy eucalypt forest, heavy scrub along creek beds and rocky mountain slopes covered with grasses. A huge 'rock lily', related to the Gymea lily of NSW, grows in abundance on the

most popular of the walks to Mt Cordeaux. Its branching flower spikes, up to 4 m tall, are covered in vivid scarlet blooms in early summer. The Spicers Gap area, reached from the eastern side of the range, has an established campsite and limited water.

The 18 400 ha park has absorbed three formerly separate parks, **Cunningham's Gap**, **Jirramun** and **Mount Roberts**, in an unbroken band of mountainous terrain reaching for more than 35 km north from the NSW border.

Abundant birdlife in the park includes bellbirds, satin bowerbirds, crimson rosellas and red-tailed black cockatoos, which feed on the profuse stands of casuarinas. Tall forest around the picnic and camping grounds supports large numbers of greater gliders, which can be spotted with the help of a strong torch as they feed in the treetops at night. Brush-tailed possums also visit the camp after dusk.

Long grasses covering the steep, rocky heights of Mt Cordeaux provide cover and den sites for the brush-tailed rock wallaby – the only wallaby species in the park likely to be encountered by day.
NOTE: Permit required for camping and fees apply.
BEST TIME: Spring, autumn.
TEL: (07) 4666 1133.
FAX: (07) 4666 1297.
ADDRESS: MS 394, Warwick 4370.

Scenic enjoyment ✔✔✔
Day activities ✔✔
Family camping ✔✔✔
Hard bushwalking ✔✔✔

17. Moogerah Peaks National Parks

100 km SW. South Coast, Curtis and Moreton weather district. Car access off Cunningham Highway via Boonah.

Rocky cliffs and peaks around Lake Moogerah dam tower over the broad expanse of Fassifern Valley and its patchwork of cultivated fields. Steep faces of sound rock fretted with narrow cracks have made the easily accessible northern peak of Mt French famous among rock climbers in Queensland. Over 150 ascent routes of varying degrees of difficulty have been established on cliffs familiarly known as Frog Buttress. On any fair weekend the climbers provide a gripping spectacle for visitors contented with easy walks through the surrounding eucalypt forest, or a drive to the lookout points in a separate section of 63 ha **Mount French National Park.**

Walking tracks have been formed and marked in two larger national parks around peaks south of Lake Moogerah. Piccabeen palms grow

profusely in one of the three main gorges at **Mount Greville** (182 ha) on a spur running off the Main Range. Rocky outcrops on steep slopes break the forest cover and views from the peak reach south to the McPherson Range.

The double peaks of **Mount Moon** form a hilly mass running south from Mt Alford in the central section of Teviot Range. White mahogany, narrow-leafed ironbark, spotted gum and yellow box cover gullies and ridges in a park of 119 ha.

The slopes of **Mount Edwards National Park** (364 ha) rise from the northern shores of Lake Moogerah. Reynolds Creek flows out of the reservoir through a wide gorge between two peaks, Mt Edwards and Little Mt Edwards, with sloping slabs of rock extending almost 1 km back from the water.
NOTE: Picnic facilities, toilets and camping only at Mt French.
BEST TIME: Spring, autumn.
TEL: (07) 5463 5041.
FAX: (07) 5463 5042.
ADDRESS: MS 3522, Ipswich-Boonah, Caulson 4310.

Scenic enjoyment ✔✔✔
Day activities ✔
Family camping ✗
Climbing ✔✔✔

18. Mooloolah River National Park

95 km N, 16 km SE of Nambour. South Coast, Curtis and Moreton weather district. Car access along unsealed road off Bruce Highway from Tanawha.

Muddy river shores backed by melaleuca swamps and marsh – the habitat of the rare ground parrot – flank eastern banks of the Mooloolah River in a park of 688 ha, less than 5 km upstream from the mouth of the river at the resort town of Mooloolaba.

Low-lying sand flats inland from the fringing belts of melaleuca support a community of wallum banksias, low scrub and heath, giving striking displays of wildflowers in spring. Light clay and standstone ridges to the north are covered with grassy eucalypt forest. The park preserves vegetation of a type fast disappearing from the coastal lowlands of southeastern Queensland.
BEST TIME: Spring, for wildflowers.
TEL: (07) 5494 3983.
FAX: (07) 5494 3986.
ADDRESS: 61 Bunya Street, Maleny 4552.
Scenic enjoyment ✔
Day activities ✔
Family camping ✗
Hard bushwalking ✗

19. Moreton Island National Park

50 km NE. South Coast, Curtis and Moreton weather district. Vehicle ferries from Redland Bay, Lytton, and Scarborough (sand tracks: suitable 4WD only). Accessible also by private boat.
DESCRIPTION: Page 57.
NOTE: All vehicles driving in the recreation area require a service permit which can be bought from barge operator. Permit required for camping and fees apply.
BEST TIME: Spring, autumn.
TEL: (07) 3408 2710.
FAX: (07) 3408 2555.
ADDRESS: c/o Tangalooma Resort, Moreton Island NP 4025.

Scenic enjoyment ✔✔
Day activities ✔✔✔
Family camping ✔✔✔
Hard bushwalking ✔✔

20. Mount Barney National Park

130 km SW of Brisbane, 14 km NE of Woodenbong. South Coast, Curtis and Moreton weather district. Follow Mt Lindesay Highway via Beaudesert to 1 km past Rathdowney, turn right on the Boonah–Rathdowney road, travel 8 km to Barney View-Upper Logan Road turnoff, then left to Yellow Pinch camping ground.

Bushwalkers gather at campsites around the Logan River in the foothills around Mt Barney (1360 m) before tackling strenuous climbs over steep sandstone ridges towards the many peaks of this 11 900 ha park. The other peaks are Mt Ernest (960 m), Mt Maroon (965 m), Mt May (839 m) and Mt Lindesay (1194 m). Creek courses – some strewn with huge boulders of coarse granite – are followed wherever possible, but in places rock walls tower over waterfalls and shallow rapids in gorges too narrow for safe passage.

Eucalypt forest of yellow stringybark, tallow wood, red bloodwood and narrow-leafed grey gum dominate the slopes of the mountainous block. Moist, sheltered gullies have luxuriant growth of shrubs and scramblers – including introduced lantana – and dense vine forest patches. Walking tracks, though not maintained, are well-defined by heavy use.

On the ridge crests eucalypts become more widely spaced above a sparse ground cover of grasses and herbs. Some high slopes are clothed in low scrub of banksia, acacia and leptospermum. Over 20 orchids have been noted on drier slopes to the east of Mt Barney.
NOTE: Camping facilities nearby at Yellow Pinch. For bush camping a permit must be booked in advance.
BEST TIME: Spring, autumn.
TEL: (07) 5463 5041.

FAX: (07) 5463 5042.
ADDRESS: MS 342, Boonah 4310.

Scenic enjoyment ✔✔✔
Day activities ✗
Family camping ✗
Walking, climbing ✔✔✔

21. Mount Mistake National Park

120 km SW, 30 km S of Laidley. South Coast, Curtis and Moreton weather district. 4WD access along rough track from Allora, 26 km N of Warwick – dry weather only. Walkers' access from south end only: from Goomburra State Forest camping ground.

Good campsites are rare on the steep slopes of the Mt Mistake Range, a spur running off the Main Range north of Cunningham's Gap. Groups are forced to pitch tents closely together in limited space.
NOTE: This is an extremely remote area, suitable only for the seasoned bushwalker.
BEST TIME: Late winter, early spring.
TEL: (07) 4666 1133.
FAX: (07) 4666 1297.
ADDRESS: As for Main Range.

Scenic enjoyment ✔✔
Day activities ✗
Family camping ✗
Hard bushwalking ✔✔

22. Noosa National Park

155 km N. South Coast, Curtis and Moreton weather district. Car access off Bruce Highway to Noosa Heads.
DESCRIPTION: Page 61.
BEST TIME: Spring, autumn.
TEL: (07) 5447 3243.
FAX: (07) 5447 2698.
ADDRESS: Park Road, Noosa Heads 4567.

Scenic enjoyment ✔✔
Day activities ✔✔
Family camping ✗
Hard bushwalking ✗

23. Sunshine Coast National Parks

91–115 km N, 15 km S–5 km N of Nambour. South Coast, Curtis and Moreton weather district. Car access off Bruce Highway between Landsborough and Kulangoor.

Four parks, **Dularcha** (138 ha), **Eudlo Creek** (39 ha), **Tucker's Creek** (53 ha) and **Ferntree Creek** (20 ha) preserve bushland flanking stretches of the Brisbane–Cairns railway from Landsborough to just north of Nambour. At Dularcha the rails were torn up after the line was diverted; walkers can follow the old track to a disused tunnel burrowing through a hillside. Tall eucalypt forest dominates the smaller parks, which remain

undeveloped – though Tucker's Creek seems destined to be surrounded by Nambour's growing suburban sprawl.
BEST TIME: Spring, autumn.
TEL: (07) 5443 8944.
FAX: (07) 5443 8942.
ADDRESS: PO Box 168, Cottontree 4558.

Scenic enjoyment ✔
Day activities ✔
Family camping ✘
Hard bushwalking ✘

24. Bribie Island National Park
77 km N. South coast, Curtis and Moreton weather district. Car access via Bruce Highway to Bribie Island turn-off, then 19 km to Bribie Bridge across Pumicestone Passage, then follow signs to Banksia Beach.

The best means of exploring this 4890 ha national park is by boat, which brings a sense of isolation and allows leisurely pursuits of birdwatching, camping, boating, picnicking and fishing.
NOTE: Campers should bring own firewood or gas bottles. Permit required for camping, fees apply.
BEST TIME: Autumn-spring.
TEL: (07) 3408 8451.
FAX: (07) 3408 8495.
ADDRESS: PO Box 324, Bribie Island 4507.

Scenic enjoyment ✔✔
Day activities ✔✔
Family camping ✔✔
Hard bushwalking ✘

25. Queen Mary Falls National Park
210 km SW, 10 km E of Killarney. Granite Belt weather district. Car access off Warwick– Legume road 4 km S of Killarney.

Headwaters of Spring Creek, a tributary of the Condamine River, churn white over a series of steep cascades before plunging vertically over the 40 m drop of Queen Mary Falls. The sound of rushing water becomes a roar as visitors make their way along the falls pathway from roomy picnic grounds at the park entrance. Guard rails line the cliff edge walk for safe but unobstructed vantage points over the waterfall, gorge and a dense wall of rainforest thriving in the persistently moist atmosphere.

Follow the circuit track through red gum forest and rainforest containing silk oak, brushbox and hoop pine, near the foot of the falls. Over one hundred bird species have been sighted in this 340 ha park.
NOTE: Camping is available adjacent to the park.
BEST TIME: Spring, autumn.
TEL: (07) 4661 3710.

FAX: (07) 4661 7001.
ADDRESS: Hermitage via Warwick 4370.

Scenic enjoyment ✔✔
Day activities ✔
Family camping ✘
Hard bushwalking ✘

26. Ravensbourne National Park
170 km W, 45 km NE of Toowoomba. South-East Coast weather district. Car access off Hampton–Esk road.

Tall red cedar, blackbean and rosewood, the grand prizes of early timber-getting, survive in this 440 ha park as superb examples of rainforest trees once common on the eastern Darling Downs. Walks ranging from a short self-guiding nature trail to half-day hikes wind through the rainforest, tall eucalypt forest on drier slopes and dense groves of piccabeen palms. Views of the Scenic Rim mountains sweep south from the higher of the park's two picnic grounds.
BEST TIME: Spring, autumn.
TEL: (07) 4698 1296.
ADDRESS: As for Crows Nest.

Scenic enjoyment ✔✔
Day activities ✔✔
Family camping ✘
Hard bushwalking ✘

27. Rocky Creek National Park
190 km SW of Brisbane, 32 km E of Warwick. Darling Downs, Maranoa weather district. Access on foot from unsealed road east of Emu Vale; turn off Cunningham Highway from Emu Vale at Warwick. Permission needed to cross private property.

An undeveloped and infrequently visited scenic reserve of 64 ha on the narrow course of Rocky Creek preserves small patches of hoop pine rainforest in the steep gullies and gorge around a double-drop waterfall of 125 m. Eucalypt forest tops a high plateau above the falls.

On the opposite side of Emu Creek there is **Merivale National Park,** a patch of untouched hill country covering 4 ha. Scrub with silky oak and white cedar grows close to the park's small creek. Ridges to the south support forest with grey gums and acacias.
BEST TIME: Spring.
TEL: (07) 4666 1133.
FAX: (07) 4666 1297.
ADDRESS: 394, Via Warwick 4370.
Scenic enjoyment ✔✔
Day activities ✘
Family camping ✘
Hard bushwalking ✘

28. Saint Helena Island National Park
7 km NE of Manly. South Coast, Curtis and Moreton weather district. Regular boat services from Breakfast Creek and Manly. Access to the historic ruins with tours run by local ranger (fees apply) or by tourist operators. Private boats may anchor in the area adjacent to the causeway.

Ruins of a prison that operated from 1867 to 1932 are preserved in Queensland's first historic site national park, covering 75 ha of low, sandy St Helena Island. The prison achieved a high degree of self-sufficiency after extensive clearing for agriculture, quarrying and building a church and a morgue. Fringing mangroves and a thin belt of forest lining the eastern shores are all that remain of St Helena's natural vegetation.
BEST TIME: Spring, autumn.
TEL: (07) 3396 5113.
FAX: (07) 3396 5715.
ADDRESS: PO Box 5066, Manly 4179.

Scenic enjoyment ✘
Day activities ✔
Family camping ✘
Hard bushwalking ✘

29. Southwood National Park
345 km W, 130 km SW of Dalby. Granite Belt weather district. Moonie Highway skirts park.

This undeveloped 7100 ha park contains an important remnant of brigalow acacia scrubland. Wilga, belah, cypress pine, casuarinas and eucalypts are intermingled with the brigalow, and in spring wildflowers colour the low shrubs and trees. Areas of rough ground with a regular pattern of depressions up to 150 cm deep are characteristic of gilgai soil formations, attributed to clays swelling and cracking during alternate wet and dry periods. Farther north, 5 km southeast of Glenmorgan, is **Erringibba National Park** (877 ha), declared in 1991; it conserves a substantial undisturbed area of brigalow, belah and yapunyah scrub.
BEST TIME: Spring.
TEL: (07) 4661 3170.
ADDRESS AND FAX: As for Bendidee.

Scenic enjoyment ✔
Day activities ✘
Family camping ✘
Hard bushwalking ✘

30. Springbrook National Park
100 km S, 20 km SW of Mudgeeraba. South Cross, Curtis and Moreton weather district. Car access: to Springbrook Plateau, 29 km from Mudgeeraba and 34

km from Nerang; to Mt Cougal, west off Gold Coast Highway to Currumbin, 21 km to end of Currumbin valley; and to Natural Bridge, 38 km from Nerang on Nerang–Murwillumbah road.

The 2620 ha park consists of three sections: Springbrook Plateau, Mt Cougal and Natural Bridge. Water is the dominant symbol in the form of waterfalls, cascades and tumbling creeks.
Springbrook Plateau. Currumbin and Nerang Creeks rise on the high ground of the plateau, just over 20 km inland. Headwaters of the streams rush down rocky courses broken by rapids and impressive cascades including the 109 m drop of Purling Brook Falls near the Gwongorella picnic area. There is a deep rock pool 1 km downstream from the base of the falls. Short tracks lead to lookouts over the falls and deep valleys and walks of 4–5 km strike out from picnic and camping grounds through rainforest festooned with vines and epiphytic orchids. The Warrie Circuit, commencing at Canyon Lookout, takes 5–6 hours.
Mount Cougal. This section of the park, at the head of the Currumbin valley, supports dense subtropical rainforest and eucalypt forest. It provides a wilderness experience for seasoned hikers prepared for strenuous climbs through trackless bush. A sealed walking track and several viewing platforms give safe access to Currumbin Creek.
Natural Bridge. This rock archway spans Cave Creek as it plunges into a deep cavern, lit at night by a colony of glow worms.
DESCRIPTION: Page 51.
NOTE: No camping in Natural Bridge or Mount Cougal sections.
BEST TIME: Spring, autumn.
TEL: (07) 5633 5147.
ADDRESS: Springbrook, via Mudgeeraba 4213.

Scenic enjoyment ✔✔✔
Day activities ✔✔✔
Family camping ✔✔
Hard bushwalking ✔

31. Sundown National Park
305 km SW, 85 km SW of Stanthorpe. Granite Belt weather district. Car access in dry conditions off Stanthorpe–Glenlyon road 15 km S of Texas turnoff. 4WD access into park's northern sections W from New England Highway at Ballandean.

The Severn River deeply dissects this 16 000 ha park on the western edge of Queensland's granite belt with a broad gorge stretching almost 20 km along its meandering course. Waters noted for their clarity are bordered by high cliffs on the outer course of river bends and densely vegetated overflow flats on the short inner curve.

Reeds grow profusely in scattered patches along quieter reaches. Forests of cypress pine and eucalypts and wide rocky outcrops cover steep gorge slopes.

Moderate rainfall and rocky soils support woodlands with dense understoreys in most of the park, though patches of vine scrub grow in deeper gorges. Small populations of superb lyrebirds and scrub turkeys occur.

Hikers follow the Severn's banks for extended walks over easy terrain, with many deeper spots in the river suitable for swimming.
NOTE: Camping requires permit, fees apply.
BEST TIME: Spring, autumn.
TEL: (02) 6737 5235.
ADDRESS: MS 312, via Stanthorpe 4390.

Scenic enjoyment ✔✔✔
Day activities ✔
Family camping ✔
Hard bushwalking ✔✔

32. Tamborine National Park
80 km S. South Coast, Curtis and Moreton weather district. Car access S of Beenleigh off Tamborine Village–Oxenford road.
DESCRIPTION: Page 52. The Tamborine park covers plots of less than 20 ha at **Tamborine Mountain** itself, **Panorama Point, Macrozamia Grove** and **MacDonald Park. Joalah** is a 38 ha park, **The Knoll** 87 ha, **Palm Grove** 118 ha, **Witches Falls** 131 ha, and the largest of the group embraces 230 ha at **Cedar Creek.**
NOTE: No picnic facilities at Joalah or Macrozamia Grove.
BEST TIME: Spring for wildflowers, autumn.
TEL: (07) 5545 1171.
ADDRESS: The Knoll Road, North Tamborine 4272.

Scenic enjoyment ✔✔✔
Day activities ✔✔
Family camping ✘
Hard bushwalking ✘

33. The Palms National Park
230 km NW, 8 km NE of Cooyar. Granite Belt weather district. Car access off New England Highway from Cooyar.

A dense grove of tall, slim-trunked piccabeen palms encloses a 500 m nature trail through this 12 ha park. Tree ferns are intermingled with the palms, and towards the grove's outer edges more complex rainforest develops.
BEST TIME: Spring, autumn.
TEL: (07) 5698 1296.
ADDRESS: As for Crows Nest.

Scenic enjoyment ✔
Day activities ✔
Family camping ✘
Hard bushwalking ✘

ROCKHAMPTON REGION

Islands and gorges on the tropical threshold

FOUNDED on the beef-fattening potential of Fitzroy Basin grasslands, Rockhampton makes no boasts as a scenic centre. Apart from some volcanic plugs and limestone formations, the district lacks distinction. But routes radiating from the riverside city put travellers within easy range of unusually varied high-country landscapes, coastal forms, islands and coral structures.

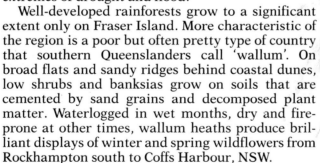

Box jellyfish

The Tropic of Capricorn, signposted on the Bruce Highway just south of Rockhampton, coincides roughly with a transition in climates. Lowlands in the north of the region have warm, dry winters, while in the south at the same time it is usually cool and damp. However the area as a whole is notorious for extremes of drought and flood.

Well-developed rainforests grow to a significant extent only on Fraser Island. More characteristic of the region is a poor but often pretty type of country that southern Queenslanders call 'wallum'. On broad flats and sandy ridges behind coastal dunes, low shrubs and banksias grow on soils that are cemented by sand grains and decomposed plant matter. Waterlogged in wet months, dry and fire-prone at other times, wallum heaths produce brilliant displays of winter and spring wildflowers from Rockhampton south to Coffs Harbour, NSW.

Travellers entering the Australian tropics for the first time should be alert to some dangers – particularly in the sea. The greatest menace, unwittingly responsible for scores of deaths, is the box jellyfish. It is most often encountered in calm nearshore waters, after local rain and when the sky is still overcast, between December and March. People are urged not to swim in summer – or if they must, to wear a T-shirt and pantyhose to limit the possible area of stinging. They should note the whereabouts of anti-venom supplies, and have a companion on watch with vinegar at hand for first-aid treatment.

On coral reefs, shoes should always be worn to guard against infectious cuts and the potentially lethal stings of cone shells or the spines of camouflaged stonefish. On muddy coasts or around river-mouths, the chances of coming upon dangerous crocodiles are slight as problem crocs in public areas are being netted and relocated. Their natural range extended at least to Tin Can Bay.

Your access and facilities guide to national parks in this region starts on page 86.

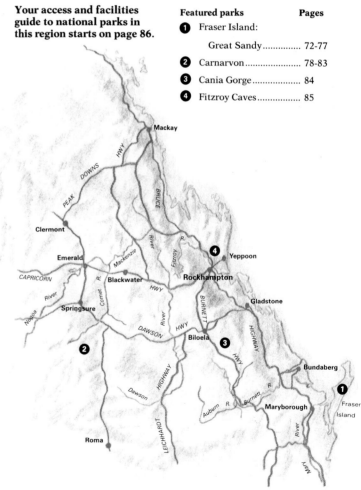

Towering sandcliffs face the Coral Sea in Great Sandy National Park

Swirling tidal action erodes a wave-cut volcanic shelf at One Tree Rocks – one of only four outcrops in a huge island of sand. Right: Waterlilies deck a brackish lagoon

FRASER ISLAND

Sediments eroded from the Great Dividing Range, then pulled by longshore currents from beaches as far south as Sydney, have accumulated in the world's biggest sand island, 120 km long and up to 22 km wide. Fraser Island's only anchors of rock are three tiny volcanic outcrops at Orchid Point, in the northeast, and one on the west coast. All the rest is sand, piling to more than 200 metres above sea level and reaching down 60 metres to the continental shelf. Nutrient salts in sea spray have fostered the germination of windborne spores and seeds carried from the mainland by birds, giving many valleys between the island's high dune ridges a deep covering of humus that supports tall rainforests. Rain soaking into the sand is held above sea level in a water table that appears at the sides of the island in gushing streams or fluctuating 'window' lakes. There are also perched lakes – rain traps with cemented beds – high among the inland dunes.

The natural balance of Fraser Island's fragile sand environment is easily disturbed; without careful management its attractions could be destroyed. It was to protect these that Fraser was declared a Recreation Area, with a board to co-ordinate policies for management and recreation. QNPWS and the Department of Forestry look after day-to-day management.

Wedding bush

Fine sands border Lake McKenzie, north of Central Station in a state forest area. Fraser Island has the world's greatest concentration of perched lakes – rain traps formed well above sea level when vegetable matter and minerals combine to cement depressions among the high dunes

FRASER ISLAND

Dense rainforest crowds a crystal clear backwater of Woongoolbver Creek, which flows west from the centre of the island to Great Sandy Strait

Left: A rotting branch adds nutrients to the richly fertile litter of a rainforest floor. Below: A staghorn attaches itself high on a tree trunk to get good light. But it is an epiphyte, not a parasite – it finds its own nourishment by trapping moisture and leaves

Piccabeen palms form an understorey for tall, vine-wreathed rainforest trees in Pile Valley, near Central Station

Bare sands of Flinders Blow, near Cape Sandy lighthouse, are pushed northwest by winds. Plants may eventually stabilise them as part of a still-growing island

Ocean Lake is the only source of fresh water along most of the eastern side of the park

GREAT SANDY NATIONAL PARK

Great Sandy was put on the map by a protracted row over Fraser Island sand mining. The 52 000 ha park occupies most of the northern third of the island, far from the mining sites. It has few of the high dune ridges, rainforested valleys and abundant streams found in the south. Camping grounds with facilities have been established at Dundubara, near the southeastern corner, at Wathumba Creek, a popular boating haven on the western side and Waddy Point, an excellent fishing area on the east coast.

Beach camping is allowed along the east coast and at some spots on the west. Areas along the beach may be closed from time to time for revegetation. There are a number of sites of historic and cultural importance along the east coast from the times when clans of the Butchulla people lived there. The park preserves eucalypt woodlands and scrubs, sandy heaths, lagoons and extensive swamps. Interesting bush and beach walks can be taken, but fresh water is scarce.

Minerals and organic staining give a multi-coloured face to the Cathedrals sandcliffs, near Dundubara camp

Plants compete in a rainforest pocket at the junction of Hell Hole and Violet Gorges

A kookaburra spies out for reptile prey above Carnarvon Creek, lined with cabbage-tree palms and casuarinas

Left: Beyond the eroding sandstone cliffs of the main gorge, seen from Boolimba Bluff lookout, a capping of basalt soils supports forests. Trees flowering in the foreground are cassinias

Native hibiscus

CARNARVON NATIONAL PARK

Carnarvon Creek cuts a 30 km gorge through outcropping sandstone, between eroded white walls that sometimes rise more than 200 metres. Tributaries feed in from narrowside chasms, dark and choked with ferns and mosses. Tall eucalypts, casuarinas, wattles, palms and cycads flourish in the main gorge, beside a waterway that has never been known to dry. The Carnarvon Range is part of Queensland's central belt of uptilted sandstone, through which rainwater seeps into the Great Artesian Basin.

A network of walking tracks, covering about 20 km, takes visitors upstream from the camping ground to all points of scenic interest – the gorge is crossed no fewer than 21 times, and a full-length return trip takes a day. Highlights such as the Moss Gardens, the Amphitheatre, Ward's Canyon, the Art Gallery and the Cathedral Cave take half a day. The Art Gallery and the Cathedral Cave are the most accessible of many caves with fine examples of Aboriginal rock painting and stencilling.

Carnarvon Gorge is the most popular section of the 298 000 ha park and has facilities for visitors. The Mt Moffatt, Salvator Rosa and Ka Ka Mundi sections are rugged and isolated, and call for bushwalking experience.

Galeola on spotted gum

Cabbage-tree palms shade the entrance to the Amphitheatre, a big opening in the south side of the gorge

CARNARVON NATIONAL PARK

Odonata, a wetlands dragonfly

Moist slime still coats a drying pool beside Mickey Creek

Algae colours the rocks of the creek bed in Ward's Canyon

Carnarvon
National
Park

*Moisture-loving plants run
riot at the Moss Gardens,
beside a gentle waterfall (far
right) in Violet Gorge*

Flattened casuarinas show the power of Carnarvon Creek in flood. Cabbage-tree palms stand out of its reach

The tree-dwelling lace monitor may grow to 2 metres. It eats eggs, insects, small mammals and other lizards

Below: Elkhorns at Bloodwood Caves cling in the crevices of bare rock, gaining their food from fallen leaf debris

Tangled rainforest growth walls off a drying pool in Russell Gully

CANIA GORGE NATIONAL PARK

Three Moon Creek creates a miniature of Carnarvon Gorge, cutting through a similar outcrop of precipice sandstone. Between walls that rise to 70 metres, subtropical rainforest plants grow beside the creek and in a maze of narrow side gullies. Outside the gorge, the park of just over 1000 ha is lightly forested with eucalypts and dry scrubs. Trails taking from 40 minutes to 6 hours return – not all of them marked – lead to lookouts and caves. As a result of a new dam, the creek is often dry. A shire-operated camping ground borders the park. Bush camping is not permitted within the park.

Deep grooves are left where trickling rainwater has dissolved soft limestone. White deposits are residues of the carbonate content of the vanished rock

FITZROY CAVES NATIONAL PARK

Dozens of caves pit a heavily eroded limestone ridge, overgrown with vine thickets among some striking sculptures of bare rock. The caves are occupied by thousands of bats, including the southernmost population of a threatened species, the ghost bat *Macroderma gigas* (picture, page 39). The colony uses different caves for different purposes. Johannsen's Cave, which is reserved for females giving birth and nursing their young, is closed to the public from June to January inclusive. It can be entered at other times, and most of the caves in a park of just over 100 ha are open year-round, but a torch and strong footwear are needed and some caves call for specialised equipment and skills. Visitors may prefer to take advantage of guided tours in privately owned caves nearby.

FACILITIES

Cabins

Caravan park

Equipped picnic area

Bush camping allowed

Lavatory building

Established campsite

Campsite but no car access

Note: Popular parks without campsites usually have public camping grounds nearby. If in doubt, call enquiries number.

PARK RATINGS: No interest ✗ Some interest ✔ Major interest ✔✔ Outstanding ✔✔✔

1. Auburn River National Park

340 km S, 42 km SW of Mundubbera. South Coast, Curtis and Moreton weather district. Car access off Burnett Highway at Mundubbera via Durong and Hawkwood roads.

Woodlands of a 390 ha park are bisected by the Auburn River, flowing in a series of cascades and rock pools. Two short walking trails in the area of the falls lead to a lookout and to the riverbank.

A long-awaited national park, **Kinkuna** (13 000 ha), with a tremendous potential for recreation focusing on the vegetation and wildlife, was created 22 km southeast of Bundaberg in 1991.

NOTE: Take drinking water. Access to camping area by 4WD only.

BEST TIME: All year.
TEL: (07) 4153 8140.
FAX: (07) 4153 8620.
ADDRESS: PO Box 1735, Bundaberg 4670.

Scenic enjoyment ✔
Day activities ✔
Family camping ✔
Hard bushwalking ✗

2. Blackdown Tableland National Park

180 km W, 55 km SE of Blackwater. Central Highlands and Central West weather district. Car access from Capricorn Highway 11 km W of Dingo. Route not suitable for caravans.

A two-part park of roughly 31 000 ha occupies an undulating sandstone plateau. The plateau, 800–950 m above sea level and generally 5°C cooler than the surrounding plains, is covered by tall, dense forest covers and cut by Mimosa Creek and its many tributaries into rugged gorges. Waterfalls drop into pools fringed with cabbage-tree palms, tree-ferns and many other ferns. Lilly-pillies grow along some creeks, and the cliffs and sandstone outcrops support elkhorns and orchids. Isolated by cliffs up to 600 m high, the tableland has many species of animals and plants that are found nowhere else. They

include a trapdoor spider, a Christmas beetle, a macrozamia cycad and a callistemon tree.

Walking tracks cover about 20 km. Climbing is not advised – the cliff edges can crumble. Several streams run throughout the year, providing pools in which walkers can cool off.

NOTES: Bookings for camping required for long weekends and school holidays. Fees apply. Bring own water.
BEST TIME: Spring, autumn.
TEL: (07) 4986 1964.
FAX: (07) 4936 2212.
ADDRESS: PO Box 3130, Rockhampton Shopping Fair 4701.

Scenic enjoyment ✔✔✔
Day activities ✔✔
Family camping ✔✔✔
Hard bushwalking ✔✔✔

3. Byfield National Park

90 km NE. Central Coast, Burdekin and Isaacs weather district. Access by 4WD off Yeppoon-Byfield road at Byfield, or by boat.

The 4090 ha park, gazetted in 1988, conserves extensive areas of frontal sand dunes, open heathlands, melaleuca swamps, clear streams and sandy beaches. Two prominent headlands, Water Park Point and Stockyard Point, add to the attractiveness and recreational potential. Ospreys nest on the windswept headland bordering Corio Bay.

Aboriginal artefacts have been found in **Mount O'Connell National Park**, a 757 ha conservation area 15km southeast of Marlborough.

BEST TIME: Autumn, spring.
TEL: (07) 4936 0511.
ADDRESS AND FAX: As for Blackdown Tableland.

4. Cania Gorge National Park

250 km SW, 100 km SE of Biloela. South Coast, Curtis and Moreton weather district. Car access off Burnett Highway 13 km NW of Monto, then 13 km along Moonford road.

DESCRIPTION: Page 84.
NOTE: Take water – tank in gorge picnic area may be empty. No

camping in the park.
BEST TIME: Spring and autumn.
TEL: (07) 4153 8140
ADDRESS AND FAX: As for Auburn River.

Scenic enjoyment ✔✔
Day activities ✔✔
Family camping ✗
Hard bushwalking ✔

5. Cape Palmerston National Park

275 km N. Central Coast, Burdekin and Isaacs weather district. 4WD access from Bruce Highway at Ilbilbie, 45 km SE of Sarina.

Diverse landforms and vegetation in this 7200 ha park include Ince Bay on the northern side of the cape, with mangroves and salt pans, hills with patches of vine forest and groves of palms, and a sandy beach facing Temple Island.

Between Cape Palmerston and Mt Funnel, a distinctively shaped volcanic plug, are expanses of gilgai ground, difficult to drive or even walk over. High rainfall and alternate wetting and drying of the soil causes areas of ground a metre or so across to rise up some 15 cm.

Freshwater lagoons, attracting many birds, are within easy walking distance of 4WD tracks.

BEST TIME: Winter (access difficult at other times).
TEL: (07) 4951 8788.
ADDRESS: PO Box 623, Mackay 4740.

Scenic enjoyment ✔✔
Day activities ✗
Family camping ✗
Hard bushwalking ✔✔

6. Capricorn Coast National Park

50 km NE. Central Coast, Burdekin and Isaacs weather district. Car access by coast road between Yeppoon and Emu Park.

The three headlands in a three-part park – Double Head, Rosslyn Head, Bluff Point – make splendid vantage points for vistas over the pretty islands in Keppel Bay. They shelter wide beaches where swimming is safe except in summer, when box jellyfish may be present.

Double Head and Rosslyn Head at the north end of one beach, Bluff Point at the other, and tiny Mulambin in the south make up the 113 ha park. On elevated parts, the wind has stunted the eucalypts; there are also heaths and mangrove flats. Walkers along tracks on Double Head and Bluff Point may spy nests of green tree ants, stitched together with leaves. Bluff Point, 121 m high, has a picnic area.

BEST TIME: Autumn, spring.
TEL: (07) 4933 6595.

FAX: (07) 4933 6619.
ADDRESS: DOE, PO Box 770, Yeppoon 4703.

Scenic enjoyment ✔✔
Day activities ✔✔
Family camping ✗
Hard bushwalking ✗

7. Carnarvon National Park

460 km SW. Central Highlands weather district. Car access to Carnarvon Gorge section off Carnarvon Developmental Road via Consuelo road 20 km S of Rolleston (may be impassable after heavy rains). 4WD access to Mt Moffatt section from Injune via Womblebank station; to Salvator Rosa section from Dawson Developmental Road through Cungelella station (inform station owners); to Ka Ka Mundi section from Dawson Developmental Road via Yandaburra station.

DESCRIPTION: Page 79. Two new national parks, **Thrushton** (25 600 ha, 132 km southwest of Roma) and **Idalia** (144 000 ha, 90 km southeast of Southall) were declared in 1990; the two properties will conserve not only vegetation as yet unrepresented in the national park estate, but an area rich in wildlife, including the rare yellow-footed rock wallaby. Yet another recently declared national park is **Chesterton Range** (16 000 ha), 25km northwest of Morven; unusual rock formations, outstanding views and interesting vegetation make the park attractive to bushwalkers and people seeking semi-wilderness experience. Another 1990 park, **Palmgrove National Park** (25 600 ha), 70 km southwest of Moura, provides protection for the poorly conserved brigalow belt; the park is of significance to Aborigines as the site of a brief battle in 1857. **Lake Nuga Nuga National Park** (2250 ha) is an important addition to the national estate in a region noted for significant Aboriginal sites; it can be reached by the Arcadia Valley Road off Dawson Highway east of Rolleston.

WARNING: Salvator Rosa and Mt Moffatt subject to heavy frosts in winter.
BEST TIME: April to October.
TEL: (07) 4982 2246 (for Carnarvon only).
FAX: (07) 4982 2359 (for Carnarvon only).
ADDRESS: Carnarvon Gorge via Rolleston 4702; Mt Moffatt via Mitchell 4465; Salvator Rosa and Ka Ka Mundi sections, PO Box 157, Springsure 4722.

Scenic enjoyment ✔✔✔
Day activities ✔✔
Family camping ✔✔✔
Hard bushwalking ✔✔✔

8. Castle Tower National Park

155 km SE. South Coast, Curtis and Moreton weather district. Car access from Bruce Highway at Iveragh siding, 30 km S of Gladstone (dirt road).

A steep granite outcrop juts from hilly woodlands of ironbark and bloodwood, cut by the headwaters of four creeks. Difficulty of access has meant the 5000 ha park is undeveloped, but it offers a challenge to experienced bushwalkers and those with a head for heights to make their way up the 550 m peak. **Rodds Peninsula National Park,** an area of 4150 ha between Tannum Sands near Gladstone and Baffle Creek, was gazetted in 1990 because of its scenic and biological values.

BEST TIME: Autumn to spring.
TEL: (07) 4972 6055.
FAX: (07) 4972 1933.
ADDRESS: DOE, PO Box 5065, Gladstone 5065.

Scenic enjoyment ✔✔
Day activities ✗
Family camping ✗
Walking, climbing ✔

9. Coalstoun Lakes National Park

360 km S, 45 km E of Gayndah. South Coast, Curtis and Moreton weather district. 4WD or foot access (3 km) from Isis Highway at Coalstoun Lakes township.

Mt LeBrun, a volcanic cone standing 200 m above surrounding farmlands, contains two connecting craters that at one time held water after rain, though no longer now. The craters are protected in a park of 26 ha.

The volcano was active until about 50 000 years ago. Pumice is found at the edges, along with basalt fragments and volcanic 'bombs' – solidified lumps of ejected lava.

BEST TIME: Year-round.
TEL: (07) 4123 7100.
ADDRESS: PO Box 101, Maryborough 4650.

Scenic enjoyment ✔
Day activities ✗
Family camping ✗
Hard bushwalking ✗

10. Dipperu National Park

330 km NW. Central Coast, Burdekin and Isaacs weather district. Car access throughout park is 4WD only; good gravel road from Peak Downs Highway, 106 km SW of Mackay.

Numerous permanent lagoons attract a great variety of birds, making the 11 100 ha park of special interest to naturalists. Among larger waterfowl, royal spoonbills, strawnecked ibis, jabirus and brolgas may be seen. Plains covered with brigalow and belah scrubs are home to grey kangaroos, swamp and black-striped wallabies, northern native 'cats' and rufous rat-kangaroos. Walking cross-country is easy, and the lagoons provide water for bush campers. But after the summer rains the main watercourse, Bee Creek, spreads to as much as 16 km wide.

BEST TIME: Spring.
TEL: (07) 4951 8788.
ADDRESS: As for Cape Palmerston.

Scenic enjoyment ✔
Day activities ✘
Family camping ✘
Hard bushwalking ✘

11. Epping Forest National Park

520 km NW, 150 km NW of Clermont Central Highlands and Central West weather district.
NO PUBLIC ACCESS.

Only scientists with official permission may visit this area of more than 2600 ha reserved to protect the sole colony of the Queensland hairy-nosed wombat. Woodlands have well-drained sandy soils – ideal for the wombats' complex burrow systems.
TEL: (07) 4933 6595.
ADDRESS: As for Capricorn Coast.

12. Eurimbula National Park

220 km SE. South Coast, Curtis and Moreton weather district. Access off Miriam Vale– Seventeen Seventy road – permit needed from QNPWS in Seventeen Seventy. Impassable after heavy rain. Boat access from Seventeen Seventy.

Beaches, creeks, swamps, estuaries and sand dunes support tropical and subtropical vegetation. Coastal forests of eucalypts and melaleucas give way to wallum heaths dominated by banksias. Moreton Bay ash is prominent in tall inland forests with understoreys of cabbage-tree palms. Vine thickets and patches of hoop pine rainforest occur on sandy soils, with piccabeen palms in the wetter tracts of rainforest. The 12 500 ha park rises no more than a few metres above sea level.

James Cook made his second Australian landing to the south at Bustard Bay. Nearby is **Round Hill National Park,** an area of some 300 ha with similar hoop pine rainforest. 4WD vehicle needed.
NOTES: Take water – creeks are tidal.
BEST TIME: Autumn to spring.
TEL: (07) 4974 9350.
FAX: (07) 4974 9400.
ADDRESS: Mail service, Agnes Water 4677.

Scenic enjoyment ✔✔
Day activities ✘
Family camping ✘
Hard bushwalking ✘

13. Fitzroy Caves National Park

22 km N. Central Coast, Burdekin and Isaacs weather district. Car or foot access by 2 km of dirt road from The Caves township on Bruce Highway.
DESCRIPTION: Page 85. The Mount Etna section of the park has been hived off and merged with Limestone Ridge National Park to form **Mount Etna Caves National Park** (391 ha), a scientific and restricted access area.
BEST TIME: Autumn to spring.
TEL: (07) 4936 0511.
ADDRESS: AS for Byfield.

Scenic enjoyment ✔
Day activities ✔

Family camping ✘
Hard bushwalking ✘

14. Great Sandy National Park

410 km SE, 70 km NE of Maryborough. South Coast, Curtis and Moreton weather district. Vehicular barge services from Riverheads to Kingfisher Bay Resort; from Riverheads to Wanggoolba; and from Urangan to Moon Point.
DESCRIPTION: Page 76. Between Fraser Island and the mainland off Urangan. **Woody** and **Little Woody Islands** (660 ha) form another national park. Accessible by boat, these rocky islands are covered in eucalypt forest with some mangrove flats. Bush camping allowed on Woody Island (no facilities – take water) but not on Little Woody Island.

1. Auburn River NP
2. Blackdown Tableland NP
3. Byfield National Park
4. Cania Gorge NP
5. Cape Palmerston NP
6. Capricorn Coast NP
7. Carnarvon NP
8. Castle Tower NP
9. Coalstoun Lakes NP
10. Dipperu NP
11. Epping Forest NP
12. Eurimbula NP
13. Fitzroy Caves NP
14. Great Sandy NP
15. Heron Island NP
16. Isla Gorge NP
17. Keppel Bay Islands NPs
18. Kroombit Tops NP
19. Litabella NP
20. Lonesome NP
21. Mazeppa NP
22. Mount Bauple NP
23. Mount Colosseum NP
24. Mount Jim Crow NP
25. Mount Walsh NP
26. Northumberland Islands NPs
27. Peak Range NP
28. Robinson Gorge (Expedition NP)
29. Simpson Desert NP
30. Snake Range NP
31. West Hill NP
32. Woodgate NP

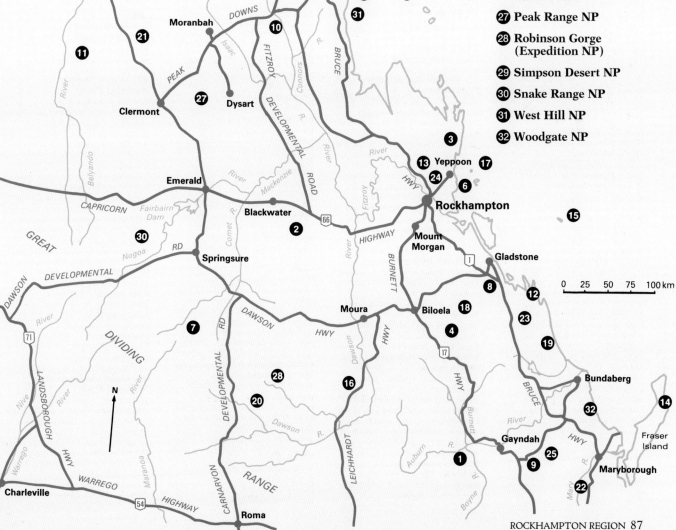

BEST TIME: May to October.
TEL: (07) 7486 3160 (Fraser Island); (07) 4123 7711 (Woody and Little Woody Islands).
ADDRESS: PO Box 30, Rainbow Beach 4581 (for Fraser Island); PO Box 101, Maryborough 4650 (Woody and Little Woody Islands).

Scenic enjoyment ✔✔✔
Day activities ✔✔
Family camping ✔✔✔
Hard bushwalking ✔✔

15. Heron Island National Park

140 km E, 70 km NE of Gladstone. Central Coast, Burdekin and Isaacs weather district. Helicopter flights from Gladstone daily; launch service six days a week.

A cay of coral debris, 17 ha in area, perches on part of an extensive reef. The national park preserves two-thirds of the cay, sharing it with a tourist resort and marine research station. Casuarina, pandanus and tournefortia trees flourish although the annual rainfall averages only about 500 mm. Inland are dense thickets of pisonia. Three turtle species, the greenback, hawksbill and loggerhead, migrate to lay their eggs in the beach sands.

Most recent of the islands of the Capricorn group to become a national park is **Wilson Island,** a sand and shingle cay of 2 ha some 15 km north of Heron Island. It is a breeding ground for roseate and black-naped terns. Other nearby park islands are **Erskine** (2 ha), **North West** and **Wreck** (111 ha) and **Tyron** (6 ha).

Three islands of the Bunker group, **Hoskyn** (8 ha), **Fairfax** (16 ha) and **Lady Musgrave** (20 ha), are national parks with special scientific status. During the nesting season of the brown gannet, from September to February, these islands may not be visited. At other times they are ideal for reef diving and snorkelling.

NOTES: Camping is permitted only on Lady Musgrave Island (except September–February; no facilities), North West Island (minimal facilities) and Tryon Island (no facilities; limit 30 campers).
BEST TIME: Autumn to spring.
TEL: (07) 4972 5690.
ADDRESS AND FAX: PO Box 5065, Gladstone 4680.
Scenic enjoyment ✔✔✔
Day activities ✔✔
Family camping ✘
Hard bushwalking ✘

16. Isla Gorge National Park

285 km S. Central Highlands and Central West weather district. Access off Leichhardt Highway 35 km S of Theodore or 55 km N of Taroom.

Steep cliffs dropping to Isla Creek can be viewed from a lookout 1.5 km from the main road along a rough track. Below are caves, arches and overhangs of sandstone, rewarding walkers who make the descent with a rich variety of forms and colours. Elsewhere the 7800 ha park is sparsely vegetated with eucalypt forest, some brigalow and bottle trees.

Close by, 50 km northeast of Taroom, is **Precipice National Park** (9050 ha, gazetted in 1989); its outstanding feature is the 10 km Dawson River frontage. Access is difficult and should not be attempted without contacting ranger in Taroom.
BEST TIME: Spring and autumn.
TEL: (07) 4627 3358.
FAX: (07) 4627 3448.
ADDRESS: PO Box 175, Taroom 4420.

Scenic enjoyment ✔
Day activities ✔✔
Family camping ✘
Hard bushwalking ✔

17. Keppel Bay Islands National Parks

60 km NE. Central Coast, Burdekin and Isaacs weather district. Launches servicing Great Keppel Island resort from Rosslyn Bay, near Yeppoon, leave campers on other islands by arrangement.

Eighteen continental islands – the peaks of coastal ranges when the sea level was lower – are grouped within 20 km of the two largest, Great and North Keppel. The bay in which they lie offers safe anchorages and calm waters over white sand, making them ideal for swimming or snorkelling. Pandanus and casuarinas behind the beaches lead to open woodland with poplar gums, bloodwoods and ironbarks.

Rising to 130 m, **North Keppel Island,** a national park of 580 ha is the largest and highest of the 11 island-parks, the others being **Corroboree Island** (20 ha), **Sloping Island** (8 ha), **Miall Island** (40 ha), **Barren Island** (81 ha), **Middle Island** (65 ha), **Halfway Island** (8 ha), **Humpy Island** (65 ha), **Pelican Island** (8 ha), **Divided Island** (8 ha), and **Peak Island** (28 ha). Middle Island has an underwater observatory and Peak Island is a restricted access area.
NOTES: North Keppel picnic area has water but campers should take their own. No water on other islands except Humpy, which has developed campsite.

BEST TIME: Autumn to spring.
TEL: (07) 4936 0511.
ADDRESS AND FAX: As for Byfield.

Scenic enjoyment ✔✔
Day activities ✔
Family camping ✔✔
Hard bushwalking ✘

18. Kroombit Tops National Park

170 km S, 60 km SW of Calliope. South Coast, Curtis and Moreton weather district. Difficult foot access from forestry road off Calliope–Monto road at Diglum Creek (obtain permit from Forestry Department at Monto).

Cliffs of the Calliope Range, up to 100 m high, overlook a park of 450 ha. It preserves a remnant of hoop pine rainforest on rough terrain, with small waterfalls fringed by ferns and palms.
BEST TIME: Spring, winter.
TEL: (07) 4936 0511.
ADDRESS AND FAX: As for Byfield.

Scenic enjoyment ✔
Day activities ✘
Family camping ✘
Walking, climbing ✔

19. Littabella National Park

230 km SE, 40 km NW of Bundaberg. South Coast, Curtis and Moreton weather district. Day access only.

Private property surrounds 2400 ha of flat heathlands bordered by a freshwater lagoon. It is an important refuge for wildlife – particularly birds – and managed as a scientific area.
TEL: (07) 4153 8140.
ADDRESS AND FAX: As for Auburn River.

20. Lonesome National Park

440 km SW via Duaringa, 510 km via Biloela. Central Highlands weather district. Car access off Carnarvon Developmental Road 85 km S of Rolleston. Arcadia Valley Road (gravel) crosses park. Creek crossings may flood.

Behind broken cliffs 200 m high, looming over the Dawson River, sandstone plateaux and ridges are wooded with eucalypts and brigalow. A lookout gives panoramic views of the 3370 ha park and the Arcadia Valley. Aptly named, the park is home to many kangaroos and wallabies.
NOTE: No water at picnic area.
WARNING: Cliff faces unstable – climbing should not be attempted.
BEST TIME: Autumn and spring.
TEL: (07) 4982 2246.
ADDRESS: As for Carnarvon Gorge.

Scenic enjoyment ✔✔
Day activities ✔
Family camping ✘
Hard bushwalking ✘

21. Mazeppa National Park

445 km NW, 75 km N of Clermont. Central Highlands and Central West weather district. Gregory Developmental Road passes boundary.

A flat 4000 ha expanse of undeveloped scrubland, set aside for scientific study, slopes gently westward to Mazeppa Creek. The scrub contains brigalow, wilga and sandalwood, but it is dominated by gidgee – a low, weeping acacia also known as stinking wattle because of the unpleasant odour it gives off at the approach of rain. The park is home to rufous bettongs, swamp wallabies, dingoes, koalas, brolgas and nankeen night herons. **Narrien National Park,** 80 km west of Clermont, protects rugged hills with ironbark woodlands and areas of lancewood.
NOTE: Permit required to camp in park. Bring own drinking water.
BEST TIME: Autumn, spring.
TEL: (07) 4982 4555.
FAX: (07) 4982 2568.
ADDRESS: PO Box 906, Emerald 4720.

Scenic enjoyment ✔
Day activities ✘
Family camping ✘
Hard bushwalking ✘

22. Mount Bauple National Park

420 km S, 35 km S of Maryborough. South Coast, Curtis and Moreton weather district. Access from Bruce Highway 32 km S of Maryborough via 2 km of rough road; very rough 4WD track in park itself.

Early confusion over placenames has left the present Mt Bauple some 2 km away. It is Mt Guyra (138 m) that dominates a park of 540 ha, its slopes covered with eucalypts, vine thickets and some hoop pine rainforest. This is a scientific park and therefore there is **NO PUBLIC ACCESS.**
BEST TIME: Year-round.
TEL: (07) 4123 7100.
FAX: (07) 4123 7150.
ADDRESS: As for Coalstoun Lakes.
Scenic enjoyment ✔
Day activities ✘
Family camping ✘
Hard bushwalking ✔

23. Mount Colosseum National Park

180 km SE. South Coast, Curtis and Moreton weather district. Car access off Bruce Highway 8 km S of Miriam Vale.

Curving spurs on the eastern face of Mt Colosseum (489 m) suggest the walls of a Roman arena. Steep slopes in the 840 ha park are forested with eucalypts and vine thickets. The summit, reached with some rock scrambling, gives views out to the Barrier Reef islands of the Capricorn and Bunker groups.
BEST TIME: Spring, autumn.
TEL: (07) 4974 9350.
ADDRESS AND FAX: As for Eurimbula.
Scenic enjoyment ✔✔
Day activities ✘
Family camping ✘
Hard bushwalking ✘

24. Mount Jim Crow National Park

30 km NE. Central Coast, Burdekin and Isaacs weather district. Rockhampton–Yeppoon road passes park.

Rising 218 m above the surrounding countryside, the volcanic plug of Jim Crow forms a conspicuous landmark. The higher slopes and the crest have few trees except for some hoop pines. Farther down, Moreton Bay figs are found among vine scrub. The flat to rolling ground of the rest of the 144 ha park supports mixed eucalypts. A track of sorts climbs to the summit, but the scrambling ascent calls for skill and fitness. Even closer to Rockhampton is **Mount Archer National Park** (1990 ha), a former environmental park that gained national park status in 1991. It is a popular venue for nature-based recreation and education; vegetation is known to total 312 species of which 16 are considered rare or endangered.
BEST TIME: Year-round.
TEL: (07) 4936 0511.
ADDRESS AND FAX: As for Fitzroy Caves.
Scenic enjoyment ✔
Day activities ✘
Family camping ✘
Hard bushwalking ✘

25. Mount Walsh National Park

350 km S. South Coast, Curtis and Moreton weather district. Access via dry weather only road off Biggenden–Maryborough road, 7 km S of Biggenden.

Eucalypt forest covers most of a rugged park of 3000 ha, with vine scrub and hoop pine on the lower eastern slopes. Mountain heaths and mallee eucalypts grow near the 645 m summit.

The peak is best suited to rock climbing, but with determination an experienced bushwalker can find a route among tumbled boulders and up gullies to the summit. About 6 hours are needed for the return trip. A creek on the west side of the mountain forms a deep swimming pool; this is difficult to find without local knowledge.

Fairlies Knob National Park preserves 40 ha of low rainforest on difficult terrain in the Sea View Range northeast of Mount Walsh.

Access is on foot up a steep track off an unsealed road north from Aramara.
NOTE: Take water when camping.
BEST TIME: Year-round.
TEL: (07) 4123 7100.
FAX: (07) 4123 7150.
ADDRESS: DOE, PO Box 101. Maryborough 4650.

Scenic enjoyment ✔
Day activities ✘
Family camping ✘
Hard bushwalking ✔

26. Northumberland Islands National Parks

150–240 km N. Central Coast, Burdekin and Isaacs weather district. Island waters accessible by boat from Mackay, but not all parks have safe landing sites.

Rocky national parks in the Northumberland chain lie undisturbed except for the infrequent visits of holidaying boat owners. Some offer safe harbour off sheltered, beach-lined bays, but many present an inaccessible cliff face, or have only the poorest of anchorage.

Slopes rise steeply from predominantly rocky shores to a height of 327 m on **Prudhoe Island** (518 ha), largest in the chain and closest to Mackay. Soils are stony with vegetation limited to tussock grassland and poorly developed vine scrub, though some hoop pines stand out. A reef-bound beach and camping ground line the island's western coast.

Flat, stony kangaroo grassland stretches between beaches on the northeastern and western shores of **Digby Island** (154 ha), largest in the Beverley group, south of Prudhoe. Boats have fair shelter here as long as seas are not too rough. Anchorage and landing sites are poor or non-existent on the smaller islands in the group: **Renou** (16 ha), **Minster** (105 ha), **Beverlac** (26 ha), **Hull** (26 ha), **Still** (8 ha), **Henderson** (53 ha), **Noel** (129 ha), **Keelan** (26 ha) and **Penn** (5 ha). Grasslands, scrub thickets, stunted eucalypts and patches of rainforest sparsely vegetate these rocky outcrops.

Bloodwoods, Moreton Bay ash and tea-tree cover **Curlew Island,** largest in the Guardfish cluster of six national park islands with a total area of 708 ha. The rocky outcrops of **Hirst, Treble, Bluff, Wallace** and **Dinner Islands** make up the rest of the group.

Two national park islands in the Percy group provide safe haven for boats towards their sheltered northwestern shores. Stunted eucalypts dominate the sparse vegetation on **North East Island** (308 ha). Eucalypt forest and some hoop pine grow on **South Island** (1619 ha), where a lagoon

surrounded by swampland provides habitats for waterbirds.
Wild Duck Island National Park (207 ha), in the North Point Isles group southwest of the Northumberlands, is one of the two known flatback turtle rookeries in eastern Australia.
BEST TIME: Spring, autumn.
TEL: (07) 4951 8788.
FAX: (07) 4951 2036.
ADDRESS: As for Cape Palmerston.

Scenic enjoyment ✔✔
Day activities ✘
Family camping ✘
Hard bushwalking ✔

27. Peak Range National Park

400 km NW. Central Highlands and Central West weather district. Car access to Gemini Mountains and Wolfang Peak beside Peak Downs Highway about 40 km NE of Clermont.

Volcanic plugs in what the explorer Ludwig Leichhardt called the Peak Range – part of the Denham Range – are reserved in a fragmented new park covering a total area of nearly 1750 ha. It includes the Gemini Mountains, Castor and Pollux, rising to 678 m on the western side of the Peak Downs Highway, Wolfang Peak about 10 km south on the other side of the highway, and Eastern Peak, well to the southeast and difficult to reach. The roadside peaks jut abruptly from sparsely wooded grasslands. Climbing involves some rock scrambling – sturdy footwear is needed. **Gemini Mountains** (787 ha) and **Wolfang Peak** (172 ha) were declared national parks in their own right in 1990; both are highly regarded for scenic and geological values.
BEST TIME: Autumn.
TEL: (07) 4982 4555.
ADDRESS AND FAX: As for Mazeppa.

Scenic enjoyment ✔✔
Day activities ✘
Family camping ✘
Walking, climbing ✔

28. Robinson Gorge Section (Expedition National Park)

445 km SW. Central Highlands and Central West weather district. Access off Leichhardt Highway 18 km N of Taroom (93 km from park). Last 15 km accessible to 4WD vehicles only. Conventional vehicles can reach the park from the north via the Bauhinia Downs–Mapala–Taroom road. Access roads impassable in wet weather.

Damp and cool, Robinson Gorge winds for over 12 km between cliffs up to 90 m high. With its side gorges – some mere fissures in the

sandstone, others wind-torn into contorted shapes – it can take days to explore. In some narrow parts visitors have to swim, or float through on inflatable mattresses. The keen-eyed find examples of Aboriginal art. Warm hues of rock belie the coolness of the narrowest sections, which the sun seldom touches.

Bottlebrushes, cabbage-tree palms, wattles and boronia flourish, and the fern gardens and moss-covered cliff bases hold special delight in their contrast to the dusty and often very hot plateau above. The whole park extends over 104 000 ha. Emus, grey kangaroos and whiptail wallabies can be seen, and dingoes occasionally venture near a camp.

From the end of the road, it is a short walk to the rim of the gorge and a scramble to the bottom. The whole park is best suited to experienced and well-equipped bushwalkers.
NOTE: Take water – creeks are seasonal and waterholes become foul and unuseable.
WARNING: Area subject to very cold weather in winter. Lack of permanent landmarks make navigation in the park difficult.
BEST TIME: Spring and autumn.
TEL: (07) 4627 3358.
ADDRESS AND FAX: As Isla Gorge.

Scenic enjoyment ✔✔✔
Day activities ✘
Family camping ✔
Hard bushwalking ✔✔

29. Simpson Desert National Park

100 km W of Birdsville. Western weather district. 4WD access from Birdsville.

Quartz sands coated with red iron oxides glow deeply at dawn and dusk in a sea of dunes running in parallel waves up to 300 km long over much of the Simpson Desert. The ridges occur every 200 to 600 m and rise to 30 m, making travel difficult and tedious, even in 4WD vehicles. Claypans and stony plains occasionally interrupt the pattern of dunes and dry salt lakes occurring in Queensland's southwestern corner and across the border in South Australia, where this 550 000 ha park is joined by an even bigger conservation park. In total the Simpson Desert is a forbidding wilderness more than twice the size of Tasmania.

Desert canegrass grows sparsely on the unstable crests and upper slopes of the dunes, with stunted gidgee woodland, scrub and hummock grass on the lower slopes and flats. Daisies, desert peas, yellowtops and many other flowering annuals have brief growing periods after rain, but

their seeds lie dormant in the sand for most of the year.

To the southeast, 35 km west of Thargomindah is **Lake Bindegolly National Park,** newly declared for the protection rare species of mulga and the birdlife associated with lakes and adjacent flats, saltpans and dunes around Lakes Bindegolly and Toomaroo. Another new national park established in 1991 is **Currawinya** (148 000 ha), near Hungerford; it lies between the Paroo River and two lakes, Wyara which is a saltwater lake and Numulla, a freshwater lake; together they provide habitats for a large variety of birds, including migratory birds.
WARNING: Visitors must be fully equipped for outback survival.
BEST TIME: Spring.
TEL: (07) 4658 1761.
FAX: (07) 4658 1860 or 4656 3249.
ADDRESS: PO Box 202, Longreach 4730.

Scenic enjoyment ✔✔
Day activities ✘
Family camping ✘
Hard bushwalking ✘

30. Snake Range National Park

400 km W, 70 km W of Springsure. Centre Highlands weather district.
NO PUBLIC ACCESS.

In an area already remote, a natural amphitheatre is further isolated by its fringe of 60 m cliffs. With a single narrow entrance through which several watercourses pass, the basin is an undisturbed area of eucalypt forest and woodland of brigalow, sandalwood and ironbark. The unusual yapunyah grows here; its leaves are eaten by koalas. Caves and overhangs of the sandstone shelter Aboriginal paintings. The 1210 ha park was created mainly to preserve the environment for scientific study.
TEL: (07) 4982 4555.
FAX: (07) 4982 2568.
ADDRESS: As for Mazeppa.

31. West Hill National Park

250 km N. Central Coast, Burdekin and Isaacs weather district. Accessible by boat only, from northern bank of West Hill creek mouth.

Low vine scrub tucked into a broad hollow behind the 680 ha park's sandy foredunes develops into patches of rainforest, with Moreton Bay figs and white cedar competing for canopy space at around 30 m. Coast banksia and Moreton Bay ash grow in a grassy forest to the west, beyond a broad corridor of grassland sparsely dotted with shrubs. Mangroves line inlets on the northern boundary.

The pyramidal peak of **West Hill Island National Park** (398 ha)

rises to the north less than 1 km offshore. Rainforest slopes fall steeply to the rocky southern shores of the island. To the north and west fine beaches fringe low-lying scrubland and a narrow spit points towards the mainland. A connecting sandbank is exposed at low tide.
BEST TIME: Spring, autumn.
TEL: (07) 4936 0511.
ADDRESS AND FAX: As for Byfield.
Scenic enjoyment ✔
Day activities ✘
Family camping ✘
Hard bushwalking ✘

32. Woodgate National Park

330 km SE. South Coast, Curtis and Moreton weather district. Car access of Bruce Highway 1 km E of Childers. 4WD needed for park tracks and to reach camping ground at Burrum River.

Close to the point where the Burrum River flows into Hervey Bay, a park of 5942 ha affords safe swimming and excellent opportunities for fishing in rivers or from the 6 km stretch of beach. Sand dunes, small swamps, mangrove flats, heaths and eucalypt forests provide a variety of habitats. Birds are prolific: more than 200 species have been recorded. Bird watchers can use a hide along a 6 km walking track. Another 6 km track has a 200 m boardwalk above a swamp.

On the opposite, southern side of the Burrum River is **Burrum River National Park,** with similar terrain and vegetation. The 1620 ha park is undeveloped. It is reached by the Burrum Heads road from the Bruce Highway. Sand tracks into the park are usable by conventional vehicles when rain has firmed the sand – otherwise 4WD is needed.
NOTE: Camping requires 4WD.
BEST TIME: Year-round (spring for wildflowers).
TEL: (07) 4126 8810 (Woodgate); 4126 8939 (Burrum River).
ADDRESS AND FAX: As for Auburn River.

Scenic enjoyment ✔✔
Day activities ✔✔
Family camping ✔✔
Hard bushwalking ✘

Plants and wildlife in Queensland parks

With 15 different natural regions within its boundaries Queensland has a greater variety of landforms, vegetation types and wildlife species than any other state. Physically it ranges from desert to reef – taking in mulga, Mitchell grass downs, brigalow, rainforest, swamp and mangrove on the way. The state has about 67 per cent of the total number of native mammal species, 80 per cent of the birds and about 56 per cent of the species of reptiles and amphibians.

Although the state is large, as more land is cleared and forest trees are felled and swamps drained, so wildlife habitat comes under threat. The 314 national parks provide a home or refuge to the whole range of Queensland wildlife. Each one also has some part of the state's wonderful diversity of plants and trees for the visitor to enjoy.

Above: The rufous bettong feeds at night on grasses and tubers which it digs up with its strongly clawed front legs

It is a lucky visitor who manages to see the rare Albert's lyrebird, here returning to feed its chick

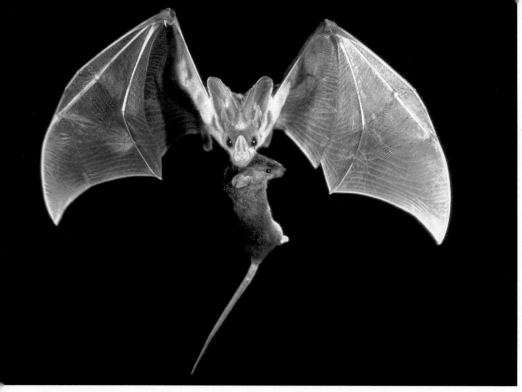

The nation's only carnivorous bat, the ghost bat Macroderma gigas, takes supper to a feeding site

Incubation period for the eggs of the emerald ground-dove is 14-16 days; it is shared by the male and female

A park inhabitant and regular visitor to Queensland gardens, a yellow-bellied sunbird feeds on grevillea. Banksia serrata, above, is a favourite food of honeyeaters

Plants and wildlife in Queensland parks

Brahminy kite – often seen along mangrove-fringed bays and inlets

The loggerhead turtle's main egg-laying season is from October to May. The loggerhead can be distinguished from other sea-turtles by the five shields on either side of its shell

As its habitat decreases with the development of the state's coastal heathlands the ground parrot is becoming increasingly rare

The delicate agile wallaby is the most common member of the kangaroo family in tropical coastal areas

Queensland's own – bottle trees make their unique mark on the landscape

Brolgas wander widely for food: although usually seen on coastal swamplands they sometimes disperse as far as the Simpson Desert

Gould's goanna is an adaptable species – its habitats range from coastal sclerophyll forest to the deserts

93

TOWNSVILLE REGION

A mighty river creates new land

YEAR BY YEAR, Bowling Green Bay National Park is growing. Just east of Townsville, it occupies part of Australia's most important river delta. Sedimentary deposits of the powerful Burdekin River form a huge triangle with the sugar town of Ayr at the centre of its 60 km base. Its apex is the long, gently curving sandspit of Cape Bowling Green. Water-saturated gravel beds underlie the triangle. South of the cape, where the surface channels of the Burdekin discharge into the Coral Sea, islands are engulfed by silt and beaches are advancing. To the west, sand flats and mangroves are claiming the bay.

Boosted by phenomenal summer rains in its main catchments – 500 km apart, near Ingham and Mackay – the Burdekin's annual outflow is the greatest of any river on the east coast. It meets a languid sea, shielded by reef ramparts that form an almost continuous barrier here. There are no strong ocean waves or currents to sweep away the river's burden of erosion debris. Sediments settle in a spreading fan. Southeasterly 'Trade Winds', blowing steadily from autumn to spring, ease sands and silts up the cape and round into the bay.

The Great Dividing Range has no influence – it retreats 200 km inland. Coastal ranges govern local climates. On each side of the Burdekin delta these ranges are set far back, and aligned southeast-to-northwest. Moisture-laden winds slip by and drop their rains towards Cairns. So although Townsville and Bowen are not spared the equatorial drenchings of summer, they share the most strongly pronounced dry season south of Cape York Peninsula. Winter and spring days are reliably sunny; nights under clear skies are surprisingly cool.

Isolated granite outcrops bring scenic relief on Townsville's lowland plain. Half an hour's drive east, the Mt Elliot massif in the inland section of the Bowling Green Bay park has rainforest of true tropical complexity – the southernmost in Australia. Others are preserved within easy reach to the north, at Mt Spec (often referred to as Crystal Creek National Park) and Jourama.

Magnetic Island, part-suburban, offers a fine sampling of drier rainforest, dominated by hoop pines and vines, among its steep eucalypt woodlands. With varied walks, sheltered swimming bays and coral formations, the island rivals many others in the region that are better publicised in the south, but far more difficult and expensive to reach.

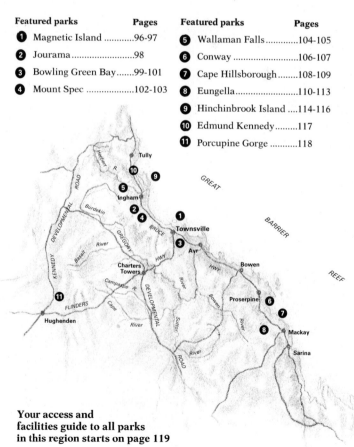

Rainforest trees crowd Finch Hatton Creek, in Eungella National Park

Your access and facilities guide to all parks in this region starts on page 119

Coral fragments lighten the granite sands of Radical Bay. The island has many fringing reefs and some offshore structures

MAGNETIC ISLAND NATIONAL PARK

Cool creek gullies lead up towards Mt Cook from a dozen quiet bays in the shelter of granite headlands. Pockets of rainforest merge into slopes of hoop pine and eucalypt woodlands studded with boulders and steep rock outcrops. More than half of the island is taken up by a national park of 2720 ha. The remainder forms part of the urban area of Townsville. Park entry points are reached along easy walking or cycling routes from ferry wharves at Picnic Bay and Arcadia.

More than 20 km of marked trails link sandy bays on the northern and eastern sides of the island with lookouts on higher ridges. Balding, Radical, Florence and Arthur Bays enjoy good reputations for swimming. Small fringing reefs of coral are common. Mt Cook (550 metres) can be climbed from north of Nelly Bay but no trail is marked; the park ranger at Picnic Bay should be consulted. Wildlife on the island includes rock wallabies, many birds, and koalas – seen most often near the Forts, above Florence Bay. The fort complex was built during World War II to protect Townsville.

Hoop pine exploits soil trapped behind a natural sea wall of boulders. These trees, related to the Norfolk Island pine and similarly salt-tolerant, grow mostly on headlands

Right: Wattles, flowering in early spring, dress the slopes above Gowrie Bay

Grassy sedges cloak a damp slope above Jourama Falls

JOURAMA FALLS

Waterview Creek tumbles over slabs of pinkish granite to a boulder-strewn bed containing many fine swimming holes. Beyond a luxuriant fringe of river plants, and some rainforest trees and shrubs in moist gullies, the granite hills of this section of Paluma Range National Park support eucalypt forests with cycads in the understorey. A track from the end of the approach road winds 1 km to the base of the main falls and zigzags for a similar distance to the lookout above. Keen bushwalkers can make a harder climb towards the source of the creek. Rock scaling is not recommended: boulders are loose in many of the faces.

Buttressed roots of many trees beside Waterview Creek show that they are rainforest species, though the canopy formed by their foliage is not dense here. Waterholes among a jumble of granite boulders offer easy opportunities for relief from the usual heat and humidity of the district

BOWLING GREEN BAY NATIONAL PARK

A steep horseshoe range, rising to 1234 metres at Mt Elliot, and two isolated coastal outliers surround Alligator Creek – the only part of a 55 000 ha wilderness accessible year-round by car. Lowland areas reach north to another granite massif at Cape Cleveland, and east across mangrove flats and salt pans to Cape Bowling Green. The highland section – formerly Mt Elliot National Park – is mostly covered by grassy eucalypt woodlands. But although the district has a generally low rainfall, the range's height and alignment enable it to catch enough moisture to support Australia's southernmost tropical rainforest. Swimming is popular at Alligator Creek; a walk to falls upstream takes 2½ hours each way.

The unadorned rock wallaby blends in with its habitat

Native rosella

Scrubs cloaking the granite bluff of Cape Ferguson compare poorly in vigour with mangrove forests at the waterline

Mangrove seedlings shoot up among oyster-encrusted rocks at Chunda Bay. Peg-like projections showing in the foreground are pneumatophores – root extensions through which plants such as mangroves take air when the tide is out

BOWLING GREEN BAY NATIONAL PARK

Crabs, yabbies, marine worms and countless smaller creatures live in mudflats fringing Bowling Green Bay. The flats, built of river silts, are still expanding. Herons and jabiru are among dozens of bird species that feed here. Brolgas breed in nearby swamps

MOUNT SPEC (PALUMA RANGE NATIONAL PARK)

Rainforests cloak the summits and much of the escarpment of the Paluma Range, above eucalypt forests with understoreys of grasses and acacias. Heights towards Mt Spec (960 metres) command fine views of the lowlands reaching to Halifax Bay, with the Palm Islands rising to the northeast. At McCleland's Lookout, near Big Crystal Creek, a track of about 1 km links picnic grounds with a series of lookouts. Longer tracks leading north and west through the range were the pack trails of tin miners in the 1920s. Little Crystal Creek, much nearer the Bruce Highway, has waterfalls, cascades and inviting swimming holes in a rainforested valley.

Green ringtail and striped possums reach the southern limit of their range here. Pademelons are likely to be seen on the Paluma Dam road, early or late in the day, and platypuses are sometimes sighted in quiet pools. Among many interesting birds are the northern log runner, the Victorian riflebird and bowerbirds.

Umbrella fern

Rainforest trees shade a little waterfall and rock pool typical of Crystal Creek. This structure may soon collapse – the rocks are cracking and seedlings are starting to widen the gaps

Fallen logs readily decompose in the high humidity of a rainforest, yielding their nutrients to support other plants. Most fertility in such forests is held above ground rather than in the soil – which is why fires can spell their doom

Youthful misfortune tied this liane in a knot. Some violent force – probably a blow from a falling branch – bent its growing tip towards the ground. Recovering, the plant turned upwards again but its shoot grew through a loop

Left: Buttress roots are characteristic of nearly all the taller trees in tropical and subtropical rainforests

Wallaman Falls' sheer drop of 279 metres is the largest permanent clear drop fall in Australia. In a process that has gone on for thousands of years, since the final uplift of the Great Dividing Range, water action is cutting back the gorge of Stony Creek deeper and deeper into the rock escarpment

WALLAMAN FALLS

The usual rule of tropical travel — avoid the summer 'Wet' — is worth breaking at Wallaman Falls. Discomforts are forgotten at the sight of Stony Creek in full flow, spilling into a precipitous canyon on its way to join the Herbert River. The total height of the falls is not the greatest in Australia — two in northern NSW exceed it — but a single sheer drop of 305 metres is unsurpassed. Other sections above the main drop, crowded by luxuriant rainforest, are impressive in their own right.

A lookout with road access commands superb views of the falls and gorge, centrepieces of a hilly park of 602 ha where forests of eucalypts and casuarinas dominate the more open slopes. A track of 4 km zigzags to the foot of the falls, past a second lookout; the walk takes about 1½ hours. A short track along Stony Creek, near the camp, reaches many good swimming holes.

Plants colonise stream-washed boulders wherever some silt collects

Right: Tree deaths in a misty rainforest above the gorge have opened the leaf canopy and allowed in more light, encouraging the vigorous growth of palm thickets

Fungi colonise a charred trunk

Volcanic rocks of the Beak, east of Shute Harbour, break down to make a shingle beach

Fruits of Guettarda speciosa

A blossom of beach hibiscus, just opening

Mangrove seedlings of two different species spring up among older plants at Shute Bay. A dozen species may be found in the one tropical mangrove community

CONWAY NATIONAL PARK

Coastal ranges reaching 560 metres, but plunging abruptly into the waters of Whitsunday Passage, dominate a largely undeveloped park of 23 800 ha. Bushwalkers on the connecting Mt Rooper and Swamp Bay tracks (7 km) gain striking views of the Whitsunday Islands. An easy circuit walk of 1 km can be taken from the camping ground near Shute Harbour, at the northern end of the park. Tall eucalypt forests on the slopes merge into lowland rainforests, with hoop pine emerging on some headlands. Possums, gliders and bandicoots are common in the bush, along with brush turkeys, scrubfowl and honeyeaters. Wading birds throng quiet bays, some of which are important as dugong and turtle breeding grounds.

Bent trunks of pandanus palm show the direction of prevailing south-easterlies

Golden orb weaver – really three times this size

Hoop pine rainforest backs the Division Rocks, which break the main beach in two

Boggy ground suits a lily

Left: A fig tree's buttress roots support an immense mass in relatively shallow soils

CAPE HILLSBOROUGH NATIONAL PARK

A steep-walled rock mass, rising to almost 300 metres, dominates the main headland of Cape Hillsborough. To the east, the spit-linked peninsulas of Andrews Point and Wedge Island form a deep curve giving shelter to narrow beaches studded with boulders. At low tide the beaches make a walking route to complement the 800 ha park's 8 km of tracks. These wander through dunes, coastal scrub, lowland hoop pine rainforest and up into grassy eucalypt forests, taking in eight lookout points. Hidden Valley has a self-guiding circuit of 2 km on which characteristic plants and animals are identified. Big brush turkeys frequent a picnic ground, and brush-tailed rock wallabies and sugar gliders may be glimpsed at night. An unformed but marked trail, taking about 6 hours and requiring fitness, leads west to Smalleys Beach. Swimming is popular in the sheltered bays except in summer, when marine stingers may be about. Then campers strike inland to a freshwater swimming hole at well-shaded Cascade Creek, which usually flows at a good level in the early months of the year.

Wedge Island, linked to Andrews Point by a shingle causeway, can be reached at low tide. In the background is Brampton Island, also a national park

EUNGELLA NATIONAL PARK

Rainforest raiders made red 'cedar' their first target. By the 1820s its timber was Australia's leading export. Later it went as furniture into grand colonial mansions and even railway carriages. Today *Toona australis* is rare, but fine examples survive on the Clarke Range at Eungella. Many are seen on the rainforest discovery walk, near Broken River camping ground, or along the Valley View track above Eungella township (pronounced Young-la).

Development in a park of nearly 50 000 ha is limited to the Eungella-Broken River-Crediton Creek area, in the southwestern corner, and Finch Hatton Gorge to the east. Together they offer a variety of forest walks of no great difficulty, 2-8 km in length, linking lookout points and good swimming spots. The rest of the park is a high and rugged wilderness where not even the most experienced bushwalkers should venture without consulting rangers.

Rough-scaled cyathea tree ferns spring up where openings in the rainforest canopy allow some direct sunlight, or filtered light all day. Right: Fruits of a rainforest solanum species – related to potatoes, eggplants and nightshades

Right: Climbers claim support from a towering tree

Casuarinas take over at the rainforest edge. About a third of the park, on drier country in the inaccessible northwest, has eucalypt forests. And Eungella has two types of rainforest. Some species high in the range, such as tulip oak, silver quandong and white beech, are not of tropical origin – they have affinities with trees now found far to the south

Cyatheas favour creekside sites at high altitude. They need mist and rain as well as some sun

Finch Hatton Creek tumbles over the Araluen Falls, following an eons-old path cut in tough igneous rock. The creek is the only known home of an amazing frog (see page 38)

Eungella National Park

Maidenhair ferns and umbrella ferns (below) need damp sites

Small herbs and ferns take advantage of extra light beside a creek near Mt Dalrymple, the highest point in the park at 1280 metres. Platypuses are frequently seen in quiet pools

Bruguiera mangrove in flower

Left: Buttress roots of a rainforest tree, slender but strong, wander far and wide to ensure it a firm anchorage

Above: The twisting root of a strangler fig descends from a host tree that may be doomed

HINCHINBROOK ISLAND NATIONAL PARK

Forests reach to the tide limit at Orchid Beach, tucked behind Cape Richards at the island's northern extremity. Boats are easily landed here and at many other spots along the sandy east coast. But stormy seas may force a long wait to get off. Cautious campers take extra supplies

Navigable channels cut the mangrove swamps of Missionary Bay. Clear beaches lie just northeast, past the forested Kirkville Hills

Peaks of Queensland's biggest and highest continental island match those of the coastal Cardwell Range, just across Hinchinbrook Channel. In fact the channel is an enormous drowned valley, now mostly clogged with mangroves. Mt Bowen (1119 metres) and two summits only slightly lower dominate the southern part of the 39 000 ha park and bring it a high rainfall that sustains dense tropical rainforests. Eucalypts take over at lower altitudes in the north, towards a boat landing at Scraggy Point, near the Haven camp. But most visitors make for a sandy, dog-leg extension jutting from the east coast. Beaches are linked by easy walking tracks and a 100 metre boardwalk crosses mangrove swamps.

HINCHINBROOK ISLAND NATIONAL PARK

*Hinchinbrook is the biggest whole-island national park
in the world. The channel separating it from the mainland is up
to 6 km wide but heavily silted and colonised by
tall mangroves, especially at the southern end. James Cook
charted 'Mt Hinchinbrook' as the summit of a ridge
that he presumed to be part of the mainland. The channel was
not discovered for a further 73 years*

EDMUND KENNEDY NATIONAL PARK

Among the swamps behind Rockingham Bay it is easy to imagine the despair of the explorer Edmund Kennedy. Put ashore in 1848 with 12 men, horses and a sheep flock, he had to reach Cape York. But in a maze of creeks and mangroves the party had to search for more than 30 km to the south to discover an inland route. Exhaustion, illness and depletion of supplies doomed the mission before any positive progress was made. Nine men were left to die along the way. Kennedy survived almost to the Cape but was speared to death by Aborigines.

Two bayside camping grounds, fairly popular in the dry season but reliant on seasonal creeks for water, are accessible in the 6200 ha park. A boardwalk is built over mangroves to the beach and a loop walking track of 2 km gives a sampling of rainforest and swampy communities of tea-tree, paperbark, fan palms and sedges. The area is an important breeding ground for waterfowl.

Woodlands of melaleuca and leptospermum surround sedge-bordered swamps of sword grass. Creek-fed, the swamps shrink in the dry season, but damp mud protects the tree roots. Other swamps are tidal and overgrown by mangroves

Serene in its sandstone canyon, Porcupine Creek creates a surprising oasis in country where good rains are unreliable

PORCUPINE GORGE NATIONAL PARK

Flat woodlands of eucalypts and acacias give no hint of the existence of Porcupine Gorge until travellers are within about 200 metres. Suddenly a gaping canyon reveals itself – relatively shallow at first in the south, but deepening and narrowing to a point at which the fissure is only 500 metres wide, but the walls are up to 150 metres high. Farther north the gorge opens out again at the Pyramids, in the area favoured by bush campers.

Porcupine Creek, flowing year-round, has penetrated a lava-flow plain of basalt and cut into underlying beds of softer sedimentary rocks. These give a rich variety of colours to the walls that tower over the watercourse with its fringing casuarinas and callistemons. Parrots abound and duck and bittern frequent the creek. Pools are suitable for swimming in autumn. The 4100 ha park has no formed tracks, but nimble visitors can enter the gorge from the Pyramid camp ground.

PARKS OF THE TOWNSVILLE REGION

1. Bladensburg National Park
630 km SW. 25 km S of Winton. Western weather district. Access via the Route of the River Gums (start 8 km from Winton on Jundah-Opalton Road).

An area of 33 700 ha next to Bladensburg station was set aside in 1984 to preserve low, flat-topped ridges of woodland, gidgee scrub and hummock grasslands, broken occasionally by denser vegetation around waterholes. The park is undeveloped.

Thistlebank National Park, 100 km north of Aramac, straddles the Torrens Creek, whose major water holes are important waterbird rookeries. The 5890 ha park was created in 1991.
BEST TIME: Winter, spring.
TEL: (07) 4657 1192.
ADDRESS: Bladensburg NP, Winton 4735.

Scenic enjoyment ✔
Day activities ✗
Family camping ✗
Hard bushwalking ✗

2. Bowling Green Bay National Park
28 km SE. North Coast, Tableland and Peninsula weather district. Car access to Mt Elliot area off Bruce Highway 24 km S of Townsville; tracks to Cape Cleveland area, off Bruce Highway 34 km S, require 4WD in wet conditions.
DESCRIPTION: Page 99.
BEST TIME: Autumn to spring.
TEL: (07) 4721 2399.
ADDRESS: PO Box 5391, Townsville 4810.

Scenic enjoyment ✔✔
Day activities ✔✔
Family camping ✔✔
Hard bushwalking ✔✔

3. Camooweal Caves National Park
1100 km W, 200 km NW of Mt Isa. Carpentaria, Gulf Rivers weather district. Car access 8 km S of Camooweal on Urandangi road. Roads impassable after rain.

The 13 800 ha that make up the park reveal little of its true nature: an elaborate cave system beneath the surface, which is still gradually enlarging as water continues to flow in from the surface and erode away the cave walls. After the summer rains the water table recedes deep in shafts leaving the caves dry and dusty for the remainder of the year. Colonies of insect-eating bats roost in the caves, emerging only after dark.
WARNING: Plan your trip carefully and be prepared for emergencies. Only experienced and properly equipped cavers should explore the caves.
BEST TIME: Winter.

FACILITIES

 Cabins
 Caravan park
 Equipped picnic area
 Bush camping allowed
 Lavatory building

Established campsite
Campsite but no car access

Note: Popular parks without campsites usually have public camping grounds nearby. If in doubt, call enquiries number.

PARK RATINGS: No interest ✗ Some interest ✔ Major interest ✔✔ Outstanding ✔✔✔

TEL: (07) 4743 2055.
FAX: (07) 4743 9800.
ADDRESS: PO Box 2316, Mount Isa 4825.

Scenic enjoyment ✔✔
Day activities ✔
Family camping ✗
Hard bushwalking ✔

4. Cape Hillsborough and Wedge Island National Park
370 km SE, 40 km NE of Mackay. Central Coast, Burdekin and Isaacs weather district. Car access off Bruce Highway from turn-offs at Mt Ossa and Yakapari.
DESCRIPTION: Page 109.
BEST TIME: Autumn, spring.
TEL: (07) 4959 0410.
ADDRESS: PO Box 623, Mackay 4740.

Scenic enjoyment ✔✔✔
Day activities ✔✔✔
Family camping ✔✔
Hard bushwalking ✔

5. Cape Upstart National Park
170 km SE, 80 km SE of Ayr. Central Coast, Burdekin and Isaacs weather district.
NO VEHICLE ACCESS.

Approached by sea, the massive weathered granite block of Cape Upstart appears as an island. The low swampy neck joining it to the mainland is invisible from a distance. Along the northern and eastern shores of the cape unbroken ramparts of rock rise steeply from the sea with acacia thickets clinging to shallow patches of soil. Low vine scrub grows in some gullies with hoop pine surviving in more moist spots.

Less forbidding shores line the western face on Upstart Bay. Narrow, rocky headlands enclose sandy beaches with inshore waters deep enough for beaching a boat. Scrub of Burdekin plum, eucalypt and pandanus grows in a narrow belt behind the beaches.
BEST TIME: Autumn to spring.
TEL: (07) 4946 7022.
ADDRESS: PO Box 332, Airlie Beach 4802.

Scenic enjoyment ✔✔
Day activities ✗
Family camping ✗
Hard bushwalking ✗

6. Conway National Park
310 km SE, 8 km E of Airlie Beach. Central Coast, Burdekin and Isaacs weather district. Car access off Bruce Highway from Proserpine. Buses Proserpine–Shute Harbour.
DESCRIPTION: Page 107.
BEST TIME: Spring.
TEL: (07) 4946 7022.
ADDRESS: PO Box 332, Airlie Beach 4802.

Scenic enjoyment ✔✔
Day activities ✔✔
Family camping ✔
Hard bushwalking ✔✔

7. Cumberland Group Island National Parks
300 km SE, 40 km NE of Mackay. Central Coast, Burdekin and Isaacs weather district. Accessible by boat. Flights and launch daily from Mackay to Brampton.

Brampton Island's 464 ha national park shares its continental island with a tourist resort that opened in 1933 as a holiday farm. Some slopes were bared by livestock, but most remain heavily forested with eucalypts. Walking tracks over hill terrain link sheltered bays with shallow, shelving beaches popular for swimming and snorkelling. Panoramic views from Brampton Peak (213 m) look out over seas studded with islands and reefs.

At very low tide visitors can wade 500 m across coral reefs and sandbanks to **Carlisle Island,** a 520 ha national park where there is an equipped campsite but no water supply. Casuarinas on sandy soils along the shoreline fringe thorn bush and dense vine scrub behind. Mangroves crowd muddy lowland areas and substantial patches of rainforest grow on sheltered slopes among tall eucalypt forests. In the absence of developed trails walkers and bush campers follow seasonal creekbeds, but some sections require clambering over boulders

and around steep cliff faces. Ferns grow towards the island's highest points, giving way to grasses on the gentle ridge line.

National parks preserve eight other islands around the same latitude as Brampton and Carlisle, ranging 90 km east to the coral cay of **Bushy Island** (2 ha). Private and chartered boats provide access to Bushy, **Penrith Island** (162 ha), **Aspatria Island** (105 ha), **Scawfell Island** (1090 ha), **Calder Island** (150 ha), **Wigton Island** (259 ha), **Cockermouth Island** (259 ha) and **Allonby Island** (36 ha).

There is an established campsite on Scawfell, bush camping only on Penrith and Cockermouth, and no camping on Wigton or Brampton. Permits are required and campers must carry plenty of water and be fully equipped for emergencies.
BEST TIME: Autumn, winter, spring.
TEL: (07) 4951 8788.
FAX: (07) 4957 2036.
ADDRESS: Box 623, Mackay 4740.
Scenic enjoyment ✔✔✔
Day activities ✔✔
Family camping ✔✔
Hard bushwalking ✔✔

8. Dryander National Park
190–220 km SE, 20 km E–50 km SE of Bowen. Central Coast, Burdekin and Isaacs weather district. Islands accessible by boat from Bowen, Dingo Beach and Airlie Beach.

Mt Dryander (820m) is the highest point on the mainland section of the park, part of a rainforest-clad range overlooking the flat sugar lands of the Proserpine River. In addition 11 inshore islands, strung in a chain from Edgecumbe Bay towards the northern entrance of Whitsunday Passage, make up the 13 000 ha park. Short, steep spurs and valleys clothed in eucalypt woodland and tussock grassland descend from the hilly backbone of Gloucester Island, the biggest in the chain. A ridge about 400 m high overlooks the sheltered anchorage at Northwest Beach where boats from Bowen are pulled ashore for picnics, swimming and camping holidays.

To the south a conical peak features prominently on the skyline of Saddleback Island. The peak is joined to a flat-topped rise at the island's northern end by a low saddle bare of vegetation. Fringing reefs of coral form an inner rubble area with patches of living coral exposed at low tide. Towards the seaward edge, where the coral is constantly below water, the patches are denser and offer rewarding snorkelling.

Thick, stunted scrub of narrow-leafed ironbark, poplar gum and bloodwood covers high, hilly Armit Island, closest to the Whitsundays.

Kangaroo and spear grasses grow on an area of level, open land near good beach landing spots on the southern shores of the island.

Gloucester, Saddleback and Armit have established camping grounds, but visitors must take sufficient water for the length of their stay. Bush camping is permitted on the undeveloped islands of the park: Gumbrell, Double Cone and Middle Islands.
BEST TIME: Autumn, spring.
TEL: (07) 4946 7022.
ADDRESS AND FAX: As for Conway.

Scenic enjoyment ✔✔
Day activities ✔
Family camping ✔✔
Hard bushwalking ✗

9. Edmund Kennedy National Park
175 km NW, 4 km N of Cardwell. North Coast, Tableland and Peninsula weather district. Car access off Bruce Highway 4 km N of Cardwell along unsealed track – impassable after heavy rains.
DESCRIPTION: Page 117.
NOTE: No fresh water in park.
BEST TIME: Autumn, spring.
TEL: (07) 4066 8601.
FAX: (07) 4066 8987.
ADDRESS: PO Box 74, Cardwell 4816.

Scenic enjoyment ✔
Day activities ✔
Family camping ✔✔
Hard bushwalking ✗

10. Eungella National Park
430 km SE, 85 km W of Mackay. Central Coast, Burdekin and Isaacs weather district. Car access off Bruce Highway from Mackay or from Mount Ossa, 46 km N of Mackay. Bus tours from Mackay.
DESCRIPTION: Page 110.
BEST TIME: Autumn to spring.
TEL: (07) 4958 4552.
ADDRESS: c/o PO, Dalrymple Heights 4757.

Scenic enjoyment ✔✔✔
Day activities ✔✔✔
Family camping ✔✔✔
Hard bushwalking ✔✔

11. Great Basalt Wall National Park
180 km SW, 100 km W of Charters Towers. Northern Tablelands weather district. Reached by road and track off Flinders Highway.

A 30 500 ha park announced in 1987, the Great Basalt Wall is evidence of the last major volcanic activity in northern Australia – it is part of a 120 km lava flow. Basalt boulders and dense vegetation form a natural wall for much of the park's boundary. It is a rough area with a confusing landscape and is suitable for experienced and

adventurous bushwalkers.
NOTE: No facilities but there is a camping reserve adjacent to the southern boundary. Bushwalkers must register with the ranger.
BEST TIME: Autumn, winter.
TEL: (07) 4787 3388.
FAX: (07) 4787 3800.
ADDRESS: PO Box 1017, Charters Towers 4820.

Scenic enjoyment ✔✔
Day activities ✔
Family camping ✘
Hard bushwalking ✔✔

① **Bladensburg NP**

② **Bowling Green Bay NP**

③ **Camooweal Caves NP**

④ **Cape Hillsborough NP**

⑤ **Cape Upstart NP**

⑥ **Conway NP**

⑦ **Cumberland Group Island NPs**

⑧ **Dryander NP**

⑨ **Edmund Kennedy NP**

⑩ **Eungella NP**

⑪ **Great Basalt Wall NP**

⑫ **Hinchinbrook Island NP**

⑬ **Jourama Falls (Paluma Range NP)**

⑭ **Lawn Hill NP**

⑮ **Magnetic Island NP**

⑯ **Mount Aberdeen NP**

⑰ **Mount Beatrice NP**

⑱ **Pioneer Peaks NP**

⑲ **Mount Fox NP**

⑳ **Mount Spec (Paluma Range NP)**

㉑ **Orpheus Island NP**

㉒ **Porcupine Gorge NP**

㉓ **Reliance Creek NP**

㉔ **Wallaman Falls**

㉕ **Whitsunday Islands NPs**

12. Hinchinbrook Island National Park

100 km NW, 6 km E of Cardwell. North Coast, Tableland and Peninsula weather district. Accessible by boat from Cardwell and Lucinda.
DESCRIPTION: Page 115.
At the southern entrance of Hinchinbrook Channel **Nypa Palms National Park** (340 ha), accessible only by boat, protects the most southerly known occurrence of nypa or mangrove palms. They grow in isolated clumps within a mixed mangrove community in the Herbert River delta. Off the northern end of Hinchinbrook Island the national parks of **Tween Brook Island** (6 ha) and **Middle Brook Island** (16 ha) are off limits to the public to protect colonies of breeding seabirds. Daily tours are run from Cardwell to **North Brook Island** (65 ha). To the northwest seasonal streams rising on a steep granite ridge flow through the poorly developed rainforest of **Goóld Island National Park** (830 ha).
BEST TIME: Winter, spring.
TEL: (07) 4066 8601.
ADDRESS AND FAX: As for Edmund Kennedy.

Scenic enjoyment ✔✔✔
Day activities ✔✔
Family camping ✔✔✔
Hard bushwalking ✔✔

13. Jourama Falls (Paluma Range National Park)

90 km NW. North Coast, Tableland and Peninsula weather district. Car access along unsealed road off Bruce Highway between Townsville and Ingham.
DESCRIPTION: Page 98.
BEST TIME: Autumn, spring.
TEL: (07) 4777 3112.
FAX: (07) 4776 3770.
ADDRESS: PO Box 1293, Ingham 4850.

Scenic enjoyment ✔✔
Day activities ✔✔
Family camping ✔
Hard bushwalking ✔

14. Lawn Hill National Park

1100 km W, 400 km N of Mt Isa. Carpentaria, Gulf Rivers weather district. Car access off Burketown–Camooweal road at Gregory Hotel 117 km S of Burketown. Roads impassable after rain. Airstrip at Adels Grove, 10 km from eastern boundary (07) 4748 5502.
Galleries of Aboriginal rock art grace the bare gorge walls of Lawn Hill Creek. Archeological excavations indicate continuous occupation of the area for more than 30 000 years. In 1991 a wilderness of 84 200 ha was added to the original 12 000 ha park.
Fan palms grow prolifically along the banks of Lawn Hill Creek in an oasis surrounded by stony plains of hummock grasses. Permanent water and good shelter attract kangaroos, emus, wallaroos and an abundant bird population. Creek banks near the camping ground fall sharply to deep clear water inhabited by tortoises and harmless freshwater crocodiles.
NOTE: Permit required for camping and fees apply.
BEST TIME: April to September.
TEL: (07) 4748 5572.
FAX: (07) 4748 5549.
ADDRESS: PMB 12, Mt Isa 4825.

Scenic enjoyment ✔✔
Day activities ✔
Family camping ✔
Hard bushwalking ✔

15. Magnetic Island National Park

10 km N, 1 km N of Picnic Bay. North Coast, Tableland and Peninsula weather district. Daily launches and vehicle ferry from Townsville.
DESCRIPTION: Page 97.
NOTE: Camping is not allowed in the park but there are campsites outside it.
BEST TIME: Autumn, spring.
TEL: (07) 4721 2399.
FAX: (07) 4771 5578.
ADDRESS: As for Bowling Green Bay.

Scenic enjoyment ✔✔✔
Day activities ✔✔✔
Family camping ✘
Hard bushwalking ✔✔

16. Mount Aberdeen National Park

250 km SE, 40 SW of Bowen. Central Coast, Burdekin and Isaacs weather district. Car access off Bowen Development Road.
Huge granite boulders strewn over steep slopes at the northern end of the Clark Range make clambering to the summit of Mt Aberdeen (990 m) a rough and strenuous climb. Forest red gum grows profusely in eucalypt woodland over much of the 2900 ha park, split into two sections around the Elliot River valley. Moist sheltered gullies support patches of low vine forest containing hoop pine.
BEST TIME: Autumn, spring.
TEL: (07) 4946 7022.
ADDRESS: As for Cape Upstart.

Scenic enjoyment ✔✔
Day activities ✘
Family camping ✘
Hard bushwalking ✔

MAJOR CHANGES
At November 1995, the protected estate of Queensland (including 211 national parks) covered 6.6 million hectares. This is 3.8 percent of the total area of the state. But the national park system is changing constantly and those intending to visit are advised to check the latest details with the Department of Environment and Heritage, the Naturally Queensland Information Centre in Brisbane, the regional offices or with the Queensland National Parks and Wildlife Service officers at the parks themselves.

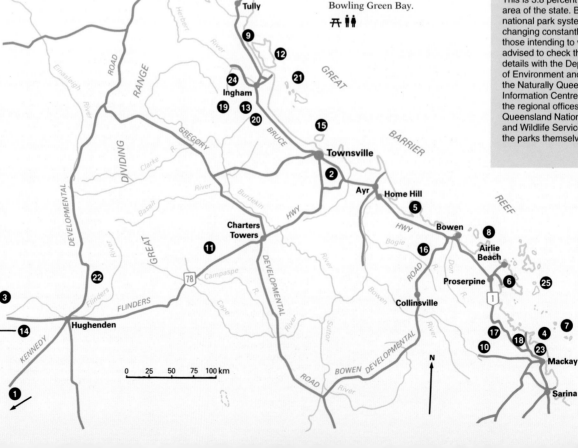

17. Mount Beatrice National Park

330 km SE, 55 km S of Proserpine. Central Coast, Burkedin and Isaacs weather district. Access on foot from Bruce Highway at Yalboroo, through private land. Permission from owner needed.

Eucalypt forest and patches of hoop pine rainforest clothe steep slopes rising to the peaks of Mt Beatrice (525 m), Mt Zillah (502 m) and Mt Catherine (476 m) in the distinct mountainous block of this 1140 ha park. Seasonal streams flow through deep gullies to lower-lying scrubland before joining Alligator Creek.

BEST TIME: Autumn, winter.
TEL: (07) 4958 4552.
FAX: (07) 4958 4501.
ADDRESS: As for Eungella.
Scenic enjoyment ✔
Day activities ✘
Family camping ✘
Hard bushwalking ✘

18. Pioneer Peaks National Park

370 km SE, 30 km NW of Mackay. Central Coast, Burdekin and Isaacs weather district. Foot access from Seaforth road off Bruce Highway at Kuttabul. Permission to cross private property must be arranged.

A television tower atop **Mt Blackwood** (590 m) stands out above a sea of low-lying sugarcane fields. Rainforest and eucalypt forest cover a 1000 ha section of park preserved from development by precipitous slopes unsuited to agriculture.

Two smaller sections preserve similar mountainous outcrops on the coastal fringe north of Mackay. Double-peaked **Mt Jukes** (547 m), just north of Mt Blackwood, carries only a sparse cover of vegetation over its 600 ha. Bare rock faces give little opportunity for plant life to develop, though some eucalypt forest and rainforest have grown on soils collected in sheltered gullies.

Mt Mandurana, also known as The Leap, rises 316 m above a small settlement on the Bruce Highway. A spur rising from the roadside provides the easiest access to a rocky peak through grassy patches, eucalypt forest and vine scrub in a park of 100 ha.

NOTE: Permit required for wilderness camping.
BEST TIME: Autumn, winter.
TEL: (07) 4959 0410.
ADDRESS: As for Cape Hillsborough.

Scenic enjoyment ✔
Day activities ✘
Family camping ✘
Hard bushwalking ✘

19. Mount Fox (Lumholtz National Park)

180 km NW, 65 km SW of Ingham. North Coast, Tableland and Peninsula weather district. Car access along unsealed road S of Trebonne, 8 km W of Ingham.

The rocky volcanic cone of Mt Fox rises to 811 m around a long-extinct crater. A thick growth of grasses masks big rocks scattered over the crater floor and makes walking difficult because of unsure footing. To the south erosion has breached the crater rim and grasses, mainly kangaroo grass, spill out over gentle slopes. Patches of low rainforest grow in moister, sheltered areas of this 200 ha section of Lumholtz NP.

NOTE: No camping; no fires.
BEST TIME: Winter, spring.
TEL: (07) 4776 1700.
FAX: (07) 4776 3770.
ADDRESS: PO Box 1293, Ingham 4850.
Scenic enjoyment ✔✔
Day activities ✘
Family camping ✘
Hard bushwalking ✘

20. Mount Spec (Paluma Range National Park)

70 km NW. North Coast, Tableland and Peninsula weather district. Car access to Little Crystal Creek and Paluma Dam off Bruce Highway 67 km N of Townsville; to Big Crystal Creek along unsealed road 69 km N.

DESCRIPTION: Page 102.
NOTE: No open fires. Bookings for campsite essential.
BEST TIME: Autumn, spring.
TEL: (07) 4776 1700.
ADDRESS AND FAX: As for Jourama.

Scenic enjoyment ✔✔✔
Day activities ✔✔✔
Family camping ✔✔
Hard bushwalking ✔

21. Orpheus Island National Park

75 km NW, 20 km SE of Lucinda. North Coast, Tableland and Peninsula weather district. Access by private or charter boat.

Cabins of a small tourist resort on Hazard Bay are backed by the low forests and grassland of this 1400 ha park. The island is 11 km long but less than 2 km at its widest, with hilly outcrops rising to around 120 m linked by narrow saddles. Eucalypts cover most of the island, interspersed with patches of tussock and rainforest in sheltered gullies. Coral reefs fringe rocky shores and strips of sandy beach popular for swimming and snorkelling.

NOTE: Camping permit must be obtained in advance. Freshwater is not available.
BEST TIME: Autumn, spring.

TEL: (07) 4776 1700.
ADDRESS: As for Mount Fox.

Scenic enjoyment ✔✔
Day activities ✔✔
Family camping ✘
Hard bushwalking ✘

22. Porcupine Gorge National Park

430 km W, 50 km N of Hughenden. Carpentaria, Gulf Rivers weather district. Car access N from Hughenden along Kennedy Developmental Road. Road impassable after heavy rains.

DESCRIPTION: Page 118. An important park, **White Mountains National Park** (55 100 ha), 80 km northeast of Hughenden, was established in 1990; its dark closed gorges, which were significant to Aboriginal people as the home of spirits with sinister powers, create an air of mystery.

BEST TIME: Autumn, spring.
TEL: (07) 4787 3388.
ADDRESS: PO Box 1017, Charters Towers 4871.

Scenic enjoyment ✔✔✔
Day activities ✔
Family camping ✘
Hard bushwalking ✔✔

23. Reliance Creek National Park

400 km SE, 10 km NW of Mackay. Central Coast, Burdekin and Isaacs weather district. Car assess from Mackay along Habana road.

Rising on the slopes of mountainous outcrops close to the coast, Reliance Creek's short course flows through a patchwork of sugarcane fields towards a mangrove-lined sea outlet. On its lower reaches the creek waters a 14 ha park around the depression of Palm Swamp. Well-developed palm-vine forest has been preserved here from the clearing and swamp drainage that has accompanied the expansion of the sugar industry.

BEST TIME: Autumn, spring.
TEL: (07) 4959 0410.
ADDRESS: As for Cape Hillsborough.
Scenic enjoyment ✔
Day activities ✘
Family camping ✘
Hard bushwalking ✘

24. Wallaman Falls

160 km NW, 50 km W of Ingham. North Coast, Tableland and Peninsula weather district. Car access along unsealed road W of Trebonne, 8 km W of Ingham.
DESCRIPTION: Page 105.
Wallaman is the only area of the Herbert River and its tributaries that has been developed and can cater for visitors. Together with the other tributaries north of

Wallaman (Yamanie, Herkes, Sword, and Garrawalt) and some further extensions, the area has now been developed to form **Lumholtz National Park,** gazetted in 1991. This new park extends from the Hinchinbrook Channel through the Herbert Valley to Princess Hills and the Herbert River Falls. It covers around 158 000 ha.

Only seasoned bushwalkers should consider exploring the area. It is not readily accessible, most waterfalls and their falls have no vehicle access and in most of them there is a high risk that walkers will meet serious difficulties. Intending visitors must get in touch with the QNPWS office in Ingham beforehand.

The area along Hinchinbrook Channel is more easily accessible; a narrow passage to the main channel winds through the mangroves from a car park and launching ramp at Fishers Creek, 28 km S of Cardwell. Swamplands and melaleuca and pandanus woodland give way to dunes covered in dense casuarina and melaleuca scrub towards the high tide line. A wide belt of mangroves and low mangrove islands clog nearshore waters.

BEST TIME: Late summer for falls viewing, spring or autumn for camping.
TEL: (07) 4776 1700.
FAX: (07) 4776 3770.
ADDRESS: PO Box 1293, Ingham 4850.

Scenic enjoyment ✔✔✔
Day activities ✔✔
Family camping ✔✔
Hard bushwalking ✔✔

25. Whitsunday Islands National Park

230–300 km SE, 50–120 km N of Mackay. Central Coast, Burdekin and Isaacs weather district. Accessible by boat from Shute Harbour, Airlie Beach, Seaforth and Mackay. Launches and charter boats from Shute Harbour and Airlie Beach; flights from Mackay and Proserpine.

Islands around Whitsunday Passage are the peaks of a mountain range that was joined to the mainland across a deep valley until it was flooded by rising sea levels. Rough, hilly terrain with precipitous cliffs and craggy peaks are striking features of the island landscapes. Drowned valleys around the big mountainous islands, Hook and Whitsunday, form fjord-like inlets capable of sheltering ocean liners. Many smaller islands have shallower bays that offer good anchorage for yachts and launches off shores lined with sandy beaches and fringing reefs of coral.

Vegetation on the island includes eucalypt forests, dense vine scrub, belts of casuarina, hoop pine rainforest and tussock grassland dotted with cycads and grass-trees.

Cruises from Mackay and Shute Harbour bring the resort island parks within easy reach for day-visit walks along extensive formed trails to quiet beaches away from the touring facilities. Established camping sites have been developed at **Whitsunday Island** (10 930 ha), **Thomas Island** (405 ha), **Henning Island** (40 ha), **North Molle Island** (259 ha), **Outer Newry Island** (58 ha), **Rabbit Island** (348 ha), and **Shute Island** (13 ha).

Popular camping grounds without facilities, but with good boat access and pleasant beachfront sites, are found on **Hook Island** (5180 ha), **Border Island** (388 ha), **Cid Island** (388 ha), **Shaw Island** (1659 ha), **Haslewood Island** (800 ha) and **Tancred Island** (6 ha). Some islands are little more than rocky outcrops of no attraction to holiday makers. Parks of less than 20 ha are on **Seaforth, Dungurra, Arkhurst, Langford, Bird, Black, Repair, Mid Molle, Planton, Denman, Nunga, Gungwiya, Yerumbinna, Wirrainbeia, Ireby, Sillago, Buddi Buddi, Pincer, Blackcombe, Acacia, Mausoleum, North Repulse, Yiundalla, Anchorsmith, Anvil, Locksmith, Bellows** and **Goat Islands,** and **Surprise Rock.**

Much better chances of shelter and a safe landing site can be expected on larger national park islands of around 20–50 ha on **Volskow, Triangle, Comston, Baynham, Gaibirra, Little Lindeman, Perseverance, Deloraine, Dumbell, Esk, Nicolson, Workington, Harold, Edward, Silversmith, Hammer, Ingot, Tinsmith, South Repulse** and **East Repulse Islands.** Largest of the undeveloped islands are **Mansell, Keyser, Maher, Pentecost, Pine, Teague, Lupton, Ladysmith** and **Blacksmith Islands** at around 100 ha, **Linne Island** (405 ha) and **Goldsmith Island** (648 ha).

NOTE: No camping in resort island parks of **Lindeman Island** (700 ha), **Newry Island** (53 ha) and **South Molle** (400 ha). There is a private camping area at **Long Island** (1030 ha). Check with ranger about availability of water at campsites; supplies must be carried to most islands.
BEST TIME: Autumn to spring.
TEL: (07) 4946 7022.
ADDRESS AND FAX: As for Conway.

Scenic enjoyment ✔✔✔
Day activities ✔✔✔
Family camping ✔✔✔
Hard bushwalking ✔

THE KILLER OF CORAL

MANY kinds of starfish eat living corals. Few of them do much damage – except for the voracious crown-of-thorns (pictured). Adults grow as big as dustbin lids, and each can bare a square metre of reef surface in a week. Local infestations hurt the tourist trade, but scientists no longer regard them with much alarm. Crown-of-thorns plagues seem to be part of a natural, recurring pattern – and damaged reefs regenerate in a few years.

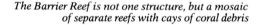

The Barrier Reef is not one structure, but a mosaic of separate reefs with cays of coral debris

An Australian Institute of Marine Science diver surveys a section of reef. Towed by a boat, he uses an aquafoil to control depth and angle of approach

Guarding an

ALL BUT 1.5 per cent of the Great Barrier Reef region is managed as a marine park. Embracing nearly 350 000 square kilometres of the waters, coral reefs and seabed off the Queensland coast between Cape York and Fraser Island, it is the biggest area of planned conservation in the world. The only exclusions are islands – many of them protected as national parks – and some inshore waters that are governed by port authorities.

Oil drilling and other mining are prohibited throughout the marine park. What else may be permitted depends on a system of zoning prescriptions. Tourist operations and commercial fishing are allowed in many zones. But where reefs are regarded as especially delicate and vulnerable, such activities are banned. Control is exercised mainly through the issue of permits specifying who can do what in a given zone, and what conditions must be met.

The Great Barrier Reef Marine Park Authority was set up by federal legislation in 1975, and the park was de-

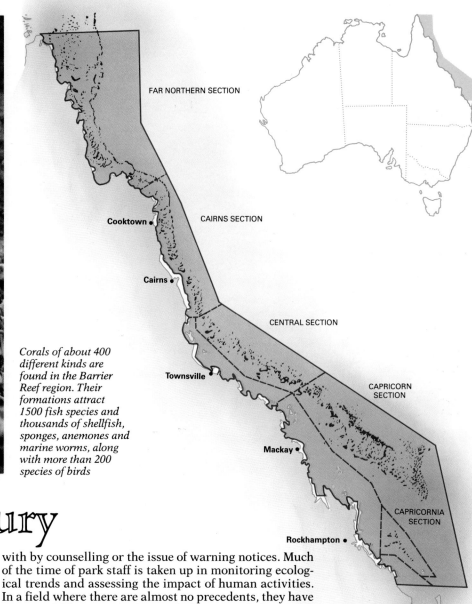

Corals of about 400 different kinds are found in the Barrier Reef region. Their formations attract 1500 fish species and thousands of shellfish, sponges, anemones and marine worms, along with more than 200 species of birds

FAR NORTHERN SECTION

CAIRNS SECTION

CENTRAL SECTION

CAPRICORN SECTION

CAPRICORNIA SECTION

Cooktown •

Cairns •

Townsville •

Mackay •

Rockhampton •

underwater treasury

clared in sectional stages between then and 1983. Planning was slow and careful because management of a marine environment is much more complicated than running a park on land. Rather than preserving tangible things that stay more or less in the same place, it is a matter of preserving processes. Some of these – fish migrations, for example – have no set geographical boundaries. Many, such as the periodic infestations by the crown-of-thorns starfish, are poorly understood.

Day-to-day management is delegated to the Queensland National Parks and Wildlife Service. Its operations have been reorganised so that the marine park and the island national parks are looked after jointly, along with some state marine parks. Compliance with zoning rules is aided by surface and aerial patrols. Air crews engaged in general coastal surveillance also send in observations.

In the park's early years, inspectors have concentrated on an educational role. Infringements are usually dealt with by counselling or the issue of warning notices. Much of the time of park staff is taken up in monitoring ecological trends and assessing the impact of human activities. In a field where there are almost no precedents, they have to see which conservation techniques work best, and whether management programmes are achieving their objectives. Among the tasks has been the tagging of thousands of reef fish to discover their movements.

Major assistance in research is provided by the federally funded Australian Institute of Marine Science, based near Townsville. Its key programmes are aimed at a better understanding of the nature of reef systems and their ecological processes. Other scientific research is conducted from four island stations spread through the reef region. Studies at Heron Island, Orpheus Island and One Tree Island are supported by the Queensland, James Cook and Sydney Universities respectively. The Australian Museum maintains a station on Lizard Island.

When fully operational, the Great Barrier Reef Marine Park will be the world's biggest zone of systematic conservation

Mountain waters bubble over the Boulders on the approach to Wooroonooran National Park

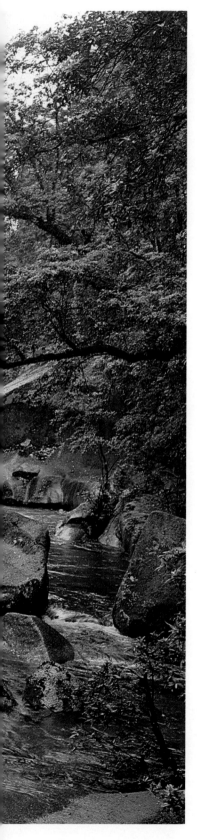

CAIRNS REGION

Rainforest relics of a vanquished kingdom

IF TREES had their own paradise, it could have been the Atherton Tableland. Two million years or more of volcanic upheavals coated it with lava to produce mineral-rich basaltic soils. Temperatures encourage year-round growth. And the cloud-shrouded peaks of the Bellenden Ker Range, beside the coast just east of the tableland, mark the region of Australia's most lavish rains.

Such perfection made it too obvious a target. Even before timber-getters could pick over the fine softwoods of the rainforests, farmers trekked up the gorges from Cairns and Innisfail to clear arable land. Gold-rush money made a ready market for their produce – and when the gold ran out the miners, too, took up farming or horticulture. Before long the forests of the coastal lowlands also disappeared, giving way to West Indian surgarcane.

What remains on the plateau, among dairy pastures, cornfields and tobacco plantations, is a scattering of patches that were too hard to lay bare. All these forest remnants are associated with bolder landforms – volcanic peaks and craters, or broken ridges and steep gorges with rushing rivers and waterfalls. So in spite of their smallness they hold exceptional scenic interest.

Most are protected now as national parks. And some are so easily reached from Cairns that half a dozen can be toured in a day – though that is too short a time to see the wildlife they harbour, let alone to take in the complexities of plant interdependence in tropical rainforests.

Not far south, in Wooroonooran National Park, bigger forests rule on steamy mountain slopes that sap the energy of any climber. To the north towards Cooktown, they have strongholds in Daintree, Dagmar Range and Cedar Bay National Parks. Access is unlikely in the summer wet season and limited at the best of times – boding well for their future as rare biological reservoirs.

Cairns flourishes as a big-game fishing base, but it has little to offer in offshore scenery. Within economical distance there is only the tiny coral cay of Green Island, its forest pathways and beaches and reef trampled and littered by 200 000 visitors a year. But the submarine world is undisturbed – and visible from a glass-walled gallery built 6 metres below the coral shelf.

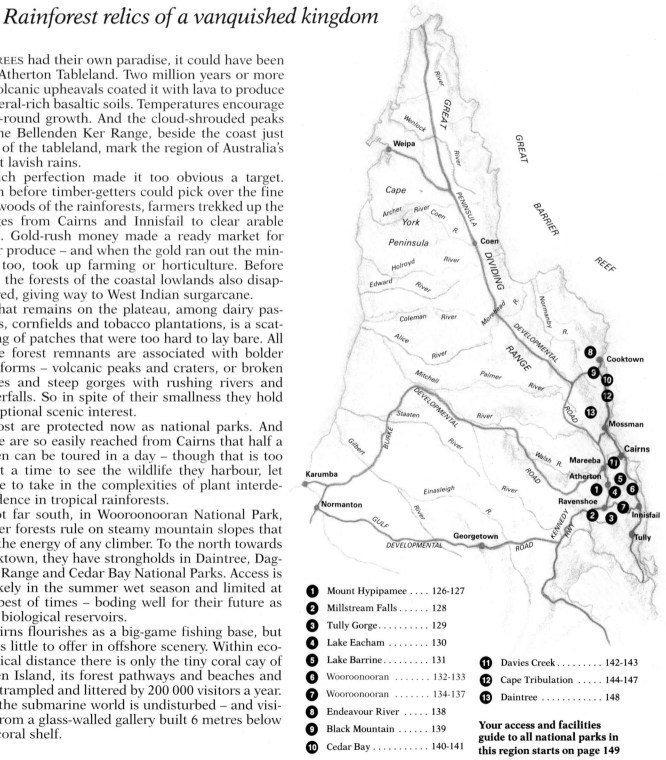

Your access and facilities guide to all national parks in this region starts on page 149

Mount Hypipamee National Park

A hole big enough to swallow a tower office block, with sheer walls plunging to a murky lake, gapes unnervingly among the rainforest of the Atherton Tableland. This cavity is a volcanic freak, with faces of granite instead of the usual basalt. Molten magma below could find no point of weakness through which to well up and build a cone. Instead its gases blasted a way out, and the rock material vanished in vapour and ash.

Towering kauri and black pine are dominant in a dense growth of rainforest trees and some eucalypts in the 360 ha park surrounding the crater. An easy track leads from picnic grounds to the crater rim. The route back passes the Barron River at Dinner Falls, where swimming is possible. Some 300 bird species frequent the area.

Staghorns are epiphytes that attach themselves to trees but live off dropped plant matter and moisture in the air

Right: Swimmers find cool refreshment at Dinner Falls, where a tributary creek spills into the Barron River

Left: Lake Hypipamee, its surface coated with algae, lies 60 metres below the crater rim. Rainforest trees (right) cloak the granite walls of the vast cavity. Fungi (above) encrusting their trunks grow profusely in warm, humid air

MILLSTREAM FALLS NATIONAL PARK

Queensland's widest waterfall - 65 metres across in full flow, and dropping 20 metres over a glistening shelf of dark basalt – makes a magnificent sight in autumn, as soon as possible after the North Queensland 'Wet' has ended. The flow continues year-round, however, even though the surrounding hills on the western slopes of the Atherton Tableland are dry and support only an open forest of eucalypts. Bottlebrush thickets border the Millstream – an important tributary of the Herbert River – on its course through the 630 ha park. Short walks are possible around the falls and the picnic ground above, and swimming is popular. Platypuses are commonly seen in placid pools above the falls, most often early or late in the day.

Lush, spray-fed plant growth protects soils above the falls from erosion by the torrential rains of the wet season

The Tully's bed is bone-dry here – but the river's former power can be seen in the cavernous cut it has made in a rainforested plateau

TULLY GORGE NATIONAL PARK

References in outdated maps and tourist guides to a Tully 'Falls' national park leads many a traveller to disappointment. Unless the gorge is seen towards the end of a heavy summer wet season, when conditions are bound to be uncomfortable, there are no waterfalls worthy of the name. At most times the flow of the Tully River is harnessed upstream by the Koombooloomba Dam, for power generation. But the 500 ha park remains impressive for its views of the steep, rainforested gorge. There is usually some river water, and a creek flows by the picnic ground. A 1.5 km track leads to a fine lookout.

LAKE EACHAM NATIONAL PARK

Lake Eacham and nearby Lake Barrine are maars – volcanic craters without cores and with little accumulation of ejected material around them. They were formed about 10 000 years ago when water trapped underground was superheated by rising magma and exploded. Eacham, 65 metres deep, covers nearly a tenth of the 490 ha rainforest park. It has no visible outflow but the level drops about 4 metres during the dry season, presumably by seepage through the crater's lower wall.

Among about 80 species of large-leafed trees surrounding the lake are several types of stinging trees; it is wise to be able to identify and so avoid these as contact with them causes a painful irritation. Marsupials are fairly active by day in the gloom under the rainforest canopy. They include the musky rat-kangaroo – smallest of the macropods and the only one with a hind-foot first toe to aid climbing. The area is a stronghold of saw-shelled tortoises, and parrots and other birds abound. But the most beautiful sight to greet visitors is likely to be that of the 10 cm Ulysses or mountain blue butterfly. A 6.5 km track encircles the lake and other paths lead to seasonal waterfalls. The lake is ideal for swimming.

Slender trees and climbers, including native monstera, crowd the crater rim

Ipomoea, a vigorous tropical climber

Left: Deep volcanic soils beside Lake Barrine support a jungle of rainforest species, with lawyer vine Calamus sp *prominent in front*

LAKE BARRINE NATIONAL PARK

Cassowaries are sometimes seen on the tracks that surround the 100 ha crater of Lake Barrine. Visitors should give them a wide berth – bigger and stronger than emus, they can inflict serious injury with their feet. Other birds of the 490 ha park include tooth-billed and satin bowerbirds, scrub fowl, brush turkeys, whipbirds, riflebirds, honeyeaters and many parrots. They have returned with the prohibition of water-skiing, which used to shatter the peace of the lake. A launch still makes scenic cruises, starting mid-morning and mid-afternoon. Swimming is popular. Walkers see most types of big rainforest trees, and in better light beside the lake there is a good chance of spotting pythons draped on the overhanging branches. They are harmless to humans.

Kauri pines, which evolved tens of millions of years before flowering trees, tower near the main lake track. They are closely related to species in New Zealand and New Caledonia. Each of this pair measures more than 6 metres around its straight bole

WOOROONOORAN NATIONAL PARK

Cycads, which recover from burning, are prominent in fire-prone foothill areas on the fringes of the rainforest. Right: Mist shrouds South Peak in the Bellenden Ker Range. Summit plants draw more moisture from mist and cloud than they do from rain

Peaks ranked along the Bellenden Ker Range are almost constantly swathed in mist or cloud. The 79 500 ha Bellenden Ker section of the park has a great span of altitude, from 80 metres above sea level by the Bruce Highway to 1622 on the domed summit of Bartle Frere, Queensland's highest mountain. Experienced bushwalkers making the 15 km ascent on the ungraded track to the summit see a transformation of forest types. Trees become shorter, their leaves smaller; the number of species and canopy layers diminishes. But ferns and orchids remain common. Above 1500 metres there is cloudforest – dense-canopied but only of scrub height. Australia's only native rhododendron grows here, flowering in the wet season when cloud cover is continuous. This section is largely undeveloped. Access for visitors not equipped for climbing is restricted to picnic areas near low-level waterfalls, where there are short walks and swimming is popular.

Palms and ferns overhang a shallow backwater of Josephine Creek. Cycad fronds (below) resemble those of palms, but the trees bear cones instead of flowers

Tough igneous boulders in Little Babinda Creek are wave-cut by a turbulent current flowing from the slopes of South Peak

Dense forest hems the fast-flowing Beatrice River, a tributary of the North Johnstone crossing the western end of the park

Below the soaking mists that cloak the Francis Range, the forest canopy seems to be impenetrable. But where there has been cyclone damage (below) more light comes in and vines compete with replacement trees

WOOROONOORAN NATIONAL PARK

Rainforest trees, although cut back when parts of the road were straightened, still wall the narrow, winding Palmerston Highway. The 14 200 ha Palmerston section of the park straddles the road for 16 km, reaching at the eastern end a pass overlooking the deep gorge of the North Johnstone River. Tracks lead down to the gorge, tributary creeks and waterfalls. There is swimming near a picnic area on Goolagan Creek and at the Henrietta Creek camping ground. Forest walks take from 30 minutes to a day.

This area receives an average annual rainfall of about 3500 mm – among the highest in Australia – concentrated between December and March. On deep, basalt-derived soils, tropical rainforest reaches the peak of its development. The section has more than 500 tree species, nearly all buttressed and vine-covered and hard to tell apart. Birds-nest and basket ferns flourish. Emerald doves and king parrots are prominent among a big population.

Crawford's Lookout commands a striking view of the North Johnstone River, surging through a sharply cut gorge. A new 500 m track leads down to the gorge

A fig tree bristles with epiphyte ferns – birdsnests, basket ferns and other species. They draw most of their moisture from the air

Wooroonooran National Park

Rhaphidophora (top left) is a hardy climber with roots that creep upwards in the grooves of tree bark. Swamp water fern (left) and club moss (above) grow closest to the edges of rivers and creeks

Across tidal mudflats, the dunes of the park are backed by a rainforested coastal range

ENDEAVOUR RIVER NATIONAL PARK

A reserve of 1840 ha extending over mudflats and sand dunes north of the Endeavour River is chiefly of historical and scientific interest. On the opposite bank in 1770 Lieut. James Cook careened his reef-holed ship for repairs, giving the botanists Joseph Banks and Daniel Solander weeks ashore for the study of Australian plants. Part of the dune area supports a tall scrub community found nowhere else. Across the river, **MT COOK NATIONAL PARK** covers nearly 500 ha on the outskirts of Cooktown. Its forested peak, rising steeply to 432 metres, dominated a watercolour by Cook's draughtsman, Sydney Parkinson – the first known Australian landscape painting.

Mangroves colonise and help to stabilise river silts in the west of the park. Their expansion is perhaps the only change since James Cook sent parties to explore the area

BLACK MOUNTAIN NATIONAL PARK

Rainforest shrubs invade wherever they find fertility

Dark lichen coats boulders of granite – some as big as houses – carried down the slopes of Black Mountain (475 metres). A park of 900 ha embraces a section of the Black Trevethan Range. The rocky summits are bare but lower slopes support shorter rainforest plants and some scattered vine thickets that are leafless in the dry season. The area was reserved principally as a habitat of Queensland rock wallabies. Just outside the park, sidetracks from the main road lead to waterfalls on the Annan River and Mumgumby Creek – best seen in autumn as soon as the Cooktown road is open.

Cedar Bay National Park

Gap Creek's clear mountain waters bisect a park of 5650 ha, affording refreshment for travellers on the rough and dusty vehicle track that follows the valley. To the west is the Finlayson Range, capped by Mt Finnigan (1148 metres). This peak gave its name to an older national park, now absorbed by Cedar Bay. Eucalypt woodlands are surmounted by rainforest, with some low cloudforest on the summits and palm thickets in creek gorges. The range is noted for the diversity of its birds and tree frogs.

A lower range to the east cuts the Gap Creek valley off from the coastal section of the park, which is more easily approached from the sea. Here mangrove flats merge into saltmarshes, paperbark swamps and finally into a lowland rainforest. The maturity and variety of its trees and vines rank it as the best forest of its type remaining anywhere south of Cooktown.

Hundreds of different rainforest species crowd untracked slopes rising to the Finlayson Range

Boulders trap river silt, allowing new trees to seed; some are lodged (right) high among buttress roots

*Gap Creek, bordered by rainforest trees and lianes, flows close by the only
vehicle track through the park. The route provides a rough link between the Cooktown
road and the Bloomfield River, where a bitterly contested road has been bulldozed
through to meet a road north from Cape Tribulation*

DAVIES CREEK NATIONAL PARK

An enormous flat granite boulder makes a perfect platform for viewing the 100 metre drop of the Davies Creek Falls. (There is a short walking track above the falls.) The stream, originating on Mt Tip Tree (1241 metres) in the Lamb Range, has a strong year-round flow through the park of 480 ha perches on the dry northwestern edge of the Atherton Tableland. Grassy eucalypt forests and woodlands, studded with grass-trees and big termite mounds, occupy broken slopes on each side of the creek. In contrast to the tree-crowded waterways of nearby rainforest parks, Davies Creek downstream of the falls has many open spots on its banks. There are good swimming holes near picnic areas. Walkers use a forestry trail, taking about 3 hours, to see more of the park.

Shelves of granite and lightly wooded slopes beside Davies Creek, below its falls, leave open areas where picnickers and swimmers enjoy winter sunshine

Right: Spray-loving shrubs and ferns overhang the foaming waters of Davies Creek Falls

Huge mounds built by colonies of grass-eating termites are common in the open woodlands

Papilio – widespread in Queensland

Rainforest reaching to the waterline at Bailey Point can be seen from Thornton Beach, a popular stop for tourist buses from Cairns

CAPE TRIBULATION

Rainforest wilderness reaches from the heights of the Thornton Range to the Coral Sea, between the Daintree and Bloomfield Rivers. but its integrity is compromised by the exclusion of many coastal sections. When a national park of 17 000 ha was proclaimed in 1981 some enclaves of settlement or other development were necessarily left out. But a long and lonely northern strip from Cape Tribulation to Bloomfield was also excised. This became the focus of heated controversy when bulldozers moved in at the end of 1983 to clear the way for a 32 km road. A conservationist protest, with some actions reminiscent of the Gordon River blockade, soon turned into a political wrangle.

Now part of Daintree National Park, this section includes the former Thornton Peak National Park, climbing to 1375 metres. Seasoned walkers can explore forests that are exceptional in their diversity of plants and wildlife. Seaside activities are concentrated outside the park.

Mt Sorrow presents a forbidding wall behind Cape Tribulation

Tangled mangroves flank Cape Tribulation Beach

Boulders of igneous rock make a platform north of Thornton Beach. The material has an exceptionally high density: when pebbles of it are thrown down they rebound back and forth. An accumulation of such pebbles on a nearby foreshore is known as the Bouncing Rocks

Cape Tribulation

Tall piccabeen palms fringe Cooper Creek, which flows out at Thornton Beach. The denser rainforest of the national park closes in behind

Right: Palms, rainforest shrubs and twining lianes compete for light in a moist gully

Among a jumble of lowland rainforest species, even the clefts of broken rocks in midstream make a seeding ground for new plants

Towards the end of the dry season, when water levels are low, the boulder-strewn bed of the Mossman River makes a path for adventurous visitors to climb the forest-hemmed gorge. There is also a short nature walk from the park's popular picnic area and swimming hole

DAINTREE NATIONAL PARK

Upland tropical rainforests and woodlands cover the steep eastern scarps of the Windsor Tableland in a wilderness park of 56 000 ha. Waterfalls spill into fast-flowing streams that feed the Daintree River. The forests are a stronghold of tree frogs, tree kangaroos, ringtail possums and the golden bowerbird, which although the smallest of its kind may build a bower 10 metres high. Only the most seasoned and self-sufficient bushwalkers penetrate much of the park. There is a 3 km walking track from the car park at the Mossman River picnic area.

PARKS OF THE CAIRNS REGION

FACILITIES

Cabins

Caravan park

Equipped picnic area

Bush camping allowed

Lavatory building

Established campsite

Campsite but no car access

Note: Popular parks without campsites usually have public camping grounds nearby. If in doubt, call enquiries number.

PARK RATINGS: No interest ✗ Some interest ✔ Major interest ✔✔ Outstanding ✔✔✔

1. Archer Bend National Park

750 km NW, 180 km NW of Coen. North Coast, Tableland and Peninsula weather district. 4WD only off Peninsula Developmental Road 107 km N of Coen via Merluna station (permission to cross station property must be pre-arranged).

Seasonal floodwaters of the Archer River spread over an alluvial plain up to 8 km wide and sweep down to the Gulf of Carpentaria with such force that patches of ground are stripped of vegetation. The river and its swamps and lagoons contain water even at the height of the dry season, supporting a diverse population of waterfowl and big numbers of freshwater crocodiles.

Rainforest crowds the riverbanks, giving way to thorn scrubs and melaleuca woodland towards the outer edges of the flood plain. Patches of grassy woodland occupy much of the northern section of this 166 000 ha park. Low sandstone ridges in the southwest support forests of eucalypt.

NOTE: Visitors must be fully equipped for outback survival.

BEST TIME: Winter.

TEL: (07) 4052 3096.

FAX: (07) 4052 3080.

ADDRESS: PO Box 2066, Cairns 4870.

Scenic enjoyment ✔
Day activities ✗
Family camping ✗
Hard bushwalking ✗

2. Barron Gorge National Park

30 km NW. North Coast, Tableland and Peninsula weather district. Car access off Kennedy Highway at Kuranda. Access to rainforest by Skyrail cableway, built in 1995.

A railway winds through rainforest and patches of eucalypt woodland in this 2800 ha park on its steep climb from Cairns to Kuranda on the Atherton Tableland. The trip is a popular tourist excursion and offers superb views of the gorge. Tinaroo Dam holds back the Barron's waters for irrigation and the flow at the falls is diverted for hydroelectric power generation. However, the falls are turned on for the tourist train and passengers are treated to the spectacle of water crashing down the 250 m drop.

BEST TIME: Winter.

TEL: (07) 4052 3096.

ADDRESS AND FAX: As for Archer Bend.

Scenic enjoyment ✔✔✔
Day activities ✔
Family camping ✗
Hard bushwalking ✔

3. Bellenden Ker (Wooroonooran NP)

60 km S. North Coast, Tableland and Peninsula weather district. Car access off Bruce Highway from turnoffs at Babinda, Pawngilly and 5 km S of Gordonvale.

DESCRIPTION: Page 132.

NOTES: Hikers should lodge their itinerary with the park ranger at Josephine Falls. Carry drinking water in winter and extra clothing to guard against sudden temperature drops at night.

WARNING: Cloud can cover the mountain peaks at short notice; care is needed to avoid getting lost.

BEST TIME: Winter.

TEL: (07) 4064 5116.

FAX: (07) 4064 5252.

ADDRESS: PO Box 93, Miriwinni 4871.

Scenic enjoyment ✔✔✔
Day activities ✔✔
Family camping ✗
Hard bushwalking ✔✔✔

4. Black Mountain National Park

305 km N, 30 km S of Cooktown. North Coast, Tableland and Peninsula weather district. Cairns–Cooktown road skirts western boundary. No camping.

DESCRIPTION: Page 139.

BEST TIME: Winter.

TEL: (07) 4052 3096.

FAX: (07) 4051 7475.

ADDRESS: As for Archer Bend.

Scenic enjoyment ✔✔
Day activities ✗
Family camping ✗
Hard bushwalking ✗

5. Cape Melville National Park

510 km NW, 200 km N of Cooktown. North Coast, Tableland and Peninsula weather district. Vehicle access via Lakefield NP or by 4WD from Cooktown north via Starcke Station. Roads impassable after heavy rains. Accessible by boat from Cooktown.

Jumbled granite boulders, some covered by black lichen, cap the Melville Range above a coast of rocky headlands and white sandy beaches lining Bathurst Bay. Vine scrub grows in hollows between the boulders and vine forest has developed on a small area of tableland.

Swamp scattered at the base of the range support palms, tea-tree and heath communities. In the south of the 137 000 ha park, slopes drop abruptly to a broad plain of eucalypt and paperbark forest interspersed with extensive areas of heath and grevillea scrubland.

Islands of the **Flinders Group National Park** (3000 ha) lie off the western end of Bathurst Bay. Sheer cliffs drop to the sea around Stanley and Flinders Islands, the two largest of the group, separated by a narrow channel and clothed in eucalypt forest. Mangroves completely cover three smaller islands.

Howick Group National Park consists of ten islands extending 20 km northwest from Coquet Island, 9 km off Murdoch Point, to Bewick Island. Most of the islands are low and wooded. The western end of the largest of them, Howick, comprises sand and coral covered with low scrub; the balance is formed of mangrove swamp. Seabirds recorded include the Torres imperial pigeon, the least frigatebird, the eastern reef heron, and the pied and sooty oystercatcher.

BEST TIME: Winter.

TEL: (07) 4052 3096.

ADDRESS AND FAX: As for Archer Bend.

Scenic enjoyment ✔✔
Day activities ✔
Family camping ✗
Hard bushwalking ✗

6. Cape Tribulation (Daintree National Park)

104 km N, 64 km N of Mossman. North Coast, Tableland and Peninsula weather district. Car access from Mossman. Vehicle ferry crosses Daintree River.

DESCRIPTION: Page 145.

NOTE: No bush camping. Permit required for camping, fees apply.

BEST TIME: Spring.

TEL: (07) 4098 0052.

FAX: (07) 4098 0074.

ADDRESS: PMB 10, PS 2041, Mossman 4873.

Scenic enjoyment ✔✔✔
Day activities ✔✔
Family camping ✗
Hard bushwalking ✔✔

7. Cedar Bay National Park

320 km N, 50 km S of Cooktown. North Coast, Tableland and Peninsula weather district. Rough track south from Cooktown via Bloomfield cuts through park. Cedar Bay itself accessible only by water. Cairns–Bloomfield about 200 km by Cape Tribulation road (4WD from Daintree ferry).

DESCRIPTION: Page 140. The **Hope Islands** to the northeast of Cedar Bay, 10 km from the coast are coral cays on the inner part of the Great Barrier Reef.

BEST TIME: Winter.

TEL: (07) 4098 0052.

FAX: (07) 4098 0074.

ADDRESS: As for Cape Tribulation.

Scenic enjoyment ✔✔✔
Day activities ✗
Family camping ✗
Hard bushwalking ✔✔

8. Chillagoe-Mungana Caves National Parks

210 km W. North Coast, Tableland and Peninsula weather district. Car access off Burke Development Road at Chillagoe, road difficult in wet conditions. Bus tours Cairns–Chillagoe most days.

Caves around the small township of Chillagoe contain fossils of coral and other marine organisms trapped about 400 million years ago when sediments covered coral reefs in a shallow sea. Earth movements lifted and tilted the limestone bed, and fault line cracks allowed fluctuating ground water levels to carve out vast chambers. Lime-bearing water constantly dripping into the caverns has created impressive formations including stalactites and stalagmites, flowstones resembling a frozen waterfall, and helictites.

Nine individual national parks preserve the formations: **Royal Arch Cave** (1514 ha), **Tower of London and Donna Caves** (178 ha), **Jubilee and Piano Caves** (126 ha), **Cathedral Cave** (20 ha), **Geck and Spring Caves** (35 ha), **Eclipse Cave** (1 ha), **Ryan Imperial Cave** (1 ha), **Markham Cave** (1 ha) and **Royal Archway Cave** (1 ha).

Daily (paying) tours guided by park rangers follow tracks through mazes of chambers and galleries at Royal Arch Cave and Donna Cave. Donna and Trezkinn Caves are electrically lit. Visitors to Royal Arch, Pompeii, Bauhinia and several others should carry battery torches. Smaller cave systems can be visited without a guide, but a strong torch is needed to supplement low filtered daylight for exploring side passages and darker recesses.

NOTE: Picnic facilities are at Royal Arch Cave.

BEST TIME: Winter.

TEL: (07) 4094 7163, 4094 7255.

FAX: (07) 4094 7213.

ADDRESS: PO Box 38, Chillagoe 4871.

Scenic enjoyment ✔✔✔
Day activities ✔✔✔
Family camping ✔✔
Hard bushwalking ✗

9. Dagmar Range (Daintree National Park)

100 km NW. North Coast, Tableland and Peninsula weather district. Mossman–Daintree road skirts eastern boundaries of the two sections of the park.

Rainforest thick with tangled vines creates a virtually impenetrable barrier on the lower slopes and in the interconnecting gullies of Dagmar Range. The forest canopy opens with the growth of tall eucalypts on higher slopes that rise to 298 m at Kilkeary Hill, above canefields and mangrove flats at the mouth of the Daintree River. Drier, flatter areas support grassy eucalypt woodlands. Intermingling of forest types on diverse landforms creates a great variety of plant cover.

A close network of ridges and streams covers the 2500 ha section, broken into two parts at the northern and southern ends of the range.

BEST TIME: Winter.

TEL: (07) 4098 2188.

ADDRESS: PO Box 251, Mossman 4873.

Scenic enjoyment ✔
Day activities ✗
Family camping ✗
Hard bushwalking ✔

10. Daintree National Park

80 km N, 5 km W of Mossman. North Coast, Tableland and Peninsula weather district. Car access to Mossman Gorge from Mossman. Unsealed road into undeveloped southwest of park off Peninsula Developmental Road 32 km north of Mount Molloy.

DESCRIPTION: Page 148.

NOTE: Camping in Cape Tribulation section only.

BEST TIME: Winter.

TEL: (07) 4098 2188.

ADDRESS: As for Dagmar Range.

Scenic enjoyment ✔✔
Day activities ✔✔
Family camping ✗
Hard bushwalking ✔✔

11. Davies Creek National Park

60 km W, 30 km S of Kuranda. North Coast, Tableland and Peninsula weather district. Car access off Kennedy Highway between Kuranda and Mareeba.
DESCRIPTION: Page 142. In 1989 a new park, **Hann Tableland** (4839 ha) was established nearby, 9 km northwest of Mareeba, accessible by a rough 4WD track off the Peninsula Development Road. It contains a prehistoric rainforest 'island', which was left isolated by climatic changes millions of years ago. There are panoramic views of distant mountains in all directions.
NOTE: Self-registration camping in Davies Creek.
BEST TIME: Winter.
TEL: (07) 4052 3096.
ADDRESS AND FAX: As for Archer Bend.

Scenic enjoyment ✔✔
Day activities ✔✔✔
Family camping ✗
Hard bushwalking ✗

12. Dunk Island (Family Islands National Park)

120 km S, 8 km SE of Clump Point. North Coast, Tableland and Peninsula weather district. Launch, water taxis and day trips from Clump Point jetty, Wongaling Beach, South Mission Beach and Mission Beach; flights from Cairns.

A forest-clad ridge forms the backbone of Dunk Island and separates the 730 ha national park from low-lying and mostly cleared ground in the western part of the island, where a busy resort complex overlooks Brammo Bay. Rainforest grows close to the water's edge, fringing a number of narrow beaches – some only accessible by boat. Walking tracks reach Mt Kootaloo (271 m) and the beach at Coconut Bay, which is as impressive as any near the resort. Walkers have a good chance of seeing the striking bright blue Ulysses butterfly.

A string of smaller islands are preserved as national parks along the coast between Mourilyan and Cardwell. They are largely undeveloped apart from some picnic areas, but many have pleasant beaches where small boats can be landed for day trips or extended camping holidays.

Kumboola Island (12 ha) and **Mung-um Nackum Island** (2 ha) are connected to Dunk by a reef, almost uncovered at low tide, and **Purtaboi Island** (6 ha) with its razorback ridges and sand flats sits off Brammo Bay to the north. **Stephens Island** (24 ha), **Sisters Island** (5 ha), **Hutchinsons Island** (19 ha) and **Jessie Island** (6 ha) in

the Barnard Group 30 km north of Dunk are continental islands covered with rainforest, melaleuca and mangrove forests. **Wheeler Island** (31 ha), **Coombe Island** (49 ha), **Smith Island** (10 ha), **Bowden Island** (10 ha) and **Hudson Island** (20 ha) in the Family Group 15 km south of Dunk are dominated by a mixture of mesophyll species with low patches of eucalypt and casuarina.
NOTES: All campers to take their own camping stoves. No wood is to be collected. Camping at Dunk Island is restricted to nine campsites each with a maximum capacity of six people. Wheeler Island is the only island of the Family Group where camping is permitted.
BEST TIME: Winter.
TEL: (07) 4066 8601.
FAX: (07) 4066 8116.
ADDRESS: PO Box 74, Cardwell 4849.

Scenic enjoyment ✔✔✔
Day activities ✔✔
Family camping ✔
Hard bushwalking ✔

13. Ella Bay and Moresby Range National Parks

Both parks 100 km S; Ella Bay 10 km NE of Innisfail, Moresby Range 10 km SE. North Coast, Tableland and Peninsula weather district. Car access to Ella Bay off Bruce Highway from Innisfail via Flying Fish Point; to Etty Bay, just outside Moresby Range park boundary, off Bruce Highway at Mourilyan.

Parts of the broken wall of low mountain ranges lining the rainforest coast east of Innisfail are preserved as national parks north and south of the Johnstone River mouth. Only determined bushwalkers make it into the forest's dense, mosquito-infested undergrowth of sharp lawyer vines and pandanus leaves.

Faint tracks attributed to the constant passage of cassowaries have been followed to the ridge top of Moresby Range where open forest clear of undergrowth allows views across lowland canefields to the west. To the east the slopes of this 240 ha park fall steeply to rocky outcrops on the shoreline.

Mt Maria, at the southern end of 3400 ha Ella Bay National Park, overlooks swampland and scattered scrub at the base of the Seymour Range.
BEST TIME: Winter.
TEL: (07) 4067 6304.
ADDRESS: Box 800, Innisfail, Qld.
Scenic enjoyment ✔
Day activities ✗
Family camping ✗
Hard bushwalking ✔

14. Endeavour River and Mount Cook National Parks

Endeavour River 340 km NW, 5 km W of Cooktown; Mount Cook 2 km SE of Cooktown. North Coast, Tableland and Peninsula weather district. Car access to both parks from Cooktown. Endeavour River accessible by boat.
DESCRIPTION: Page 138.
BEST TIME: Winter.
TEL: (07) 4052 3096.
ADDRESS AND FAX: As for Archer Bend.
Scenic enjoyment ✔
Day activities ✗
Family camping ✗
Hard bushwalking ✔

15. Eubenangee Swamp National Park

80 km S, 16 km NW of Innisfail. North Coast, Tableland and Peninsula weather district. Car access off Bruce Highway from Miriwinni.

A 1.5 km walking track follows the eastern margin of the park, allowing visitors to explore Eubenangee's fascinating wetland landscape. It skirts the edge of the Alice River before ascending grassland to the top of a solitary hill, giving views of Mt Bartle Frere to the west and swamplands extending in all directions.

The 1520 ha park is an important refuge for birdlife, particularly the waterfowl that flock to it during inland dry periods. The stately, black-necked stork (or jabiru) nests in the park every year. Herons, egrets, ibis, spoonbills and ducks are commonly seen feeding in the swamplands. The best spot to watch these waterbirds is the grassy hill. Freshwater crocodiles inhabit the swamp throughout the year. Basket ferns and orchids are among the epiphytic plants that cling to the branches of paperbarks. Rainforest, strewn with fallen logs and rocks covered in mosses, liverworts and lichen, grows in patches along creeks feeding the swamp, but a tangle of vines makes hard going even on the shortest of walks.
BEST TIME: Winter.
TEL: (07) 4052 3096.
FAX: (07) 4052 6443.
ADDRESS: Box 93, Minwinni 4871.
Scenic enjoyment ✔✔
Day activities ✔
Family camping ✗
Hard bushwalking ✗

16. Forty Mile Scrub National Park

240 km SW, 65 km SW of Mount Garnet. North Coast, Tableland and Peninsula weather district. Kennedy Highway passes through the park.

White cedar, coffee senna and poison peach, growing along the road margins of this 4600 ha park are among the species that have

been quickest to reclaim land cleared during construction of the Kennedy Highway. Behind them, low dry scrub of Burdekin plum, kurrajong and bottle tree is distinguished by an understorey of turkey bush, and thickets of hard, corky-barked vines. Red-legged pademelons and black-striped wallabies use the thickets as shelter from the fierce daytime heat. Grassy eucalypt woodland and some ironbark forest surround the scrubland.

Near Mount Surprise, 40 km to the east of the park is a new 597 ha national park, **Undara Crater,** gazetted in 1989. The crater is the source point of a lava flow that has created a 65 km system of huge, tube-like caves. It is the longest lava flow in Australia and one of the longest in the world. Rainforest scrub covers the sides of the crater and the caves are an important roosting and nursery site for several bat species.

Visitors to Forty Mile Scrub NP are advised to park off the edge of the road and view the scrub on foot. No facilities are available, so bring own drinking water.
BEST TIME: Winter.
TEL: (07) 4095 3768.
ADDRESS AND FAX: As for Lake Eacham.
Scenic enjoyment ✔
Day activities ✗
Family camping ✗
Hard bushwalking ✗

17. Frankland Group National Park

45 km SE, 20 km NE of Bramston Beach. North Coast, Tableland and Peninsula weather district. Boat access from Deeral.

White sandy beaches and shady eucalypt forests make the national park islands in the Frankland group popular destinations for picnic trips from the small resort of Bramston Beach. **Normanby Island** (6 ha), **High Island** (69 ha), **Mabel Island** (2 ha), and **Round Island** (1 ha), all undeveloped, are easily reached by boat and have fringing reefs of coral which delight snorkellers.
BEST TIME: Winter.
TEL: (07) 4052 3096.
ADDRESS AND FAX: As for Archer Bend.

Scenic enjoyment ✔✔
Day activities ✔✔
Family camping ✗
Hard bushwalking ✗

18. Graham Range National Park

70 km SE, 19 km NE of Miriwinni. North Coast, Tableland and Peninsula weather district. 4WD only along rough track from Bramston Beach, 12 km off Bruce Highway at Miriwinni.

Beach ridges and swales support forest of casuarinas, melaleucas and acacias at the base of steep slopes rising to around 700 m near Mt Josey in the northern block of the Graham Range. Paperbarks and pandanus grow thickly in swampland behind the coastal ridges, protecting an isolated occurrence of pitcher plants, normally found on swamp margins north of Coen on Cape York Peninsula, over 500 km away. North of the swamp a small area of grassland is hemmed in by the predominant rainforest vegetation of the 2900 ha park. Vines, particularly species of calmus, grow vigorously throughout the forest and acacias occur increasingly towards the summit of the range.

River and estuary areas flanking the park to the west and north are preserved as national parks in **Russell River** (350 ha) and **Mutchero Inlet** (450 ha). Palm vine forests, mangroves and low melaleuca forest dominate wetlands best reached by canoe or dinghy.
BEST TIME: Winter.
TEL: (07) 4067 6304.
ADDRESS: As for Bellenden Ker.

Scenic enjoyment ✔✔
Day activities ✗
Family camping ✗
Hard bushwalking ✗

19. Green Island National Park

30 km NE. North Coast, Tableland and Peninsula weather district. Daily boat services from Cairns.

Coral cay development at Green Island is seen at a highly advanced stage. Casuarinas, pandanus and tournefortias fringe the 12 ha island, enclosing vegetation similar to mainland rainforest but lacking its diversity – there are only 40-odd species. Fine sands of reef debris ring the island with superb beaches. On the windward southeast corner they are cemented to form exposed masses of beach rock.

Walking tracks wind through the 7 ha national park forest, but most interest on the island is generated by the displays of a small resort, and the 500 ha marine park reef around the cay. An observatory 6 m below sea level allows viewing of underwater reef life. Walks over the reef can be taken at low tide; in addition glass-bottom boats make frequent trips each day.

Tree cover is not yet established on the two cays of **Michaelmas and Upolu Cays National Park** (3 ha), northeast of Green Island. The cays are at an early stage of development with only a thin covering of coarse grasses and hardy creepers nourished by the

1 Archer Bend NP

2 Barron Gorge NP

3 Bellenden Ker
(Wooroonooran NP)

4 Black Mountain NP

5 Cape Melville NP

6 Cape Tribulation
(Daintree NP)

7 Cedar Bay NP

8 Chillagoe-Mungana
Caves NPs

9 Dagmar Range
(Daintree NP)

10 Daintree NP

11 Davies Creek NP

12 Dunk Island
(Family Islands NP)

13 Ella Bay and Moresby
Range NPs

14 Endeavour River and
Mount Cook NPs

15 Eubenangee
Swamp NP

16 Forty Mile Scrub NP

17 Frankland Group NPs

18 Graham Range NP

19 Green Island NP

20 Grey Peaks NP

21 Hasties Swamp NP

22 Hull River NP

23 Iron Range NP

24 Jardine River NP

25 Kurrimine NP

26 Lake Barrine
(Crater Lakes NP)

27 Lake Eacham
(Crater Lakes NP)

28 Lakefield NP

29 Lizard Island NP

30 Maria Creek and
Clump Mountain NPs

31 Millstream Falls NP

32 Mitchell and Alice
Rivers NP

33 Mount Hypipamee NP

34 Mount Major
(Tully Gorge NP)

35 Palmerston
(Wooroonooran NP)

36 Possession Island NP

37 Rokeby NP

38 Staaten River NP

39 Starcke NP

40 Topaz Road NP

41 Tully Gorge NP

MAJOR CHANGES
At November 1995, the
protected estate of Queensland
(including 211 national parks)
covered 6.6 million hectares.
This is 3.8 percent of the total
area of the state. But the
national park system is
changing constantly and
those intending to visit are
advised to check the latest
details with the Department
of Environment and Heritage,
the Naturally Queensland
Information Centre in Brisbane,
the regional offices or with the
Queensland National Parks
and Wildlife Service officers at
the parks themselves.

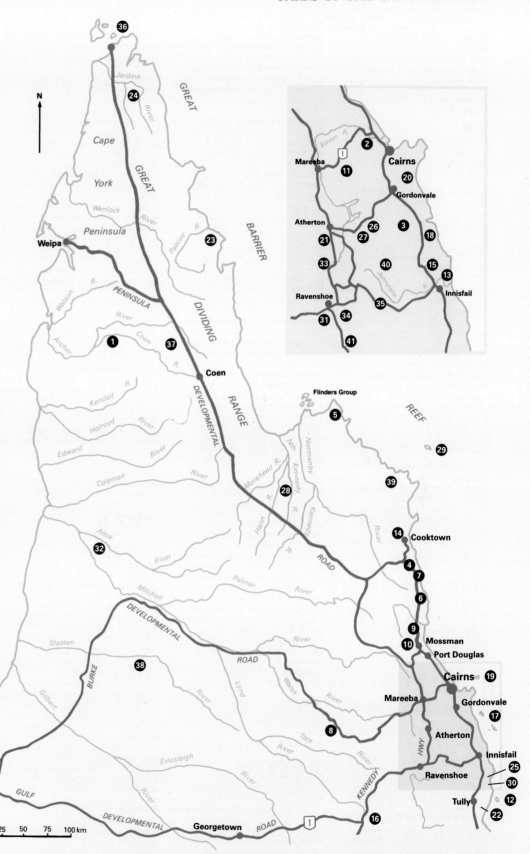

droppings of thousands of seabirds, predominantly sooty terns and crested terns, breeding in dense colonies.
BEST TIME: Winter.
TEL: (07) 4052 3096.
ADDRESS AND FAX: As for Archer Bend.

Scenic enjoyment ✔✔✔
Day activities ✔✔✔
Family camping ✘
Hard bushwalking ✘

20. Grey Peaks National Park

30 km S. North Coast, Tableland and Peninsula weather district. No vehicle access. Park approached on foot from Yarrabah road off Bruce Highway at Kamma.

Trackless rainforest with fan palms and emergent eucalypts clothes the Grey Peaks ridge, rising to 250 m at the northern end of the Malbon Thompson Range. Bushwalkers find their own way into the 900 ha park through open areas scattered with trees and patches of forest.
BEST TIME: Winter.
TEL: (07) 4052 3096.
ADDRESS AND FAX: As for Archer Bend.

Scenic enjoyment ✔
Day activities ✘
Family camping ✘
Hard bushwalking ✔

21. Hasties Swamp National Park

85 km SW, 4 km S of Atherton. North Coast, Tableland and Peninsula weather district. Car access off Herberton road from Atherton.

Preservation of this 60 ha swamp has secured an important habitat and breeding ground for a great diversity of waterfowl species. The area was once a camping and water reserve, but activities have been limited with the declaration of the national park to minimise disturbance to the birds.
BEST TIME: Winter.
TEL: (07) 4095 3768.
ADDRESS AND FAX: As for Lake Eacham.
Scenic enjoyment ✔
Day activities ✔
Family camping ✘
Hard bushwalking ✘

22. Hull River National Park

155 km S, 15 km E of Tully. North Coast, Tableland and Peninsula weather district. Car access along tracks from Lower Tully off Bruce Highway 5 km S of Tully. Access via walking trail from South Mission Beach.

Slopes around Mt Tam O'Shanter fall gently from high foothills covered with vine forest through tall grassy eucalypt woodland to

paperbark woodland on low-lying and poorly drained coastal soils. Waterfowl breed in sedge-lined swamps around the base of the hills. Creek rising around Mt Tam O'Shanter and Mt Mackay wind through the mangrove flats of the 3070 ha park to join the Hull and North Hull Rivers on their courses to Kennedy Bay. River Rat boat tours from Mission Beach.
NOTE: No camping allowed.
BEST TIME: Winter.
TEL: (07) 4068 7183.
ADDRESS: PO Box 89, Mission Beach 4854.

Scenic enjoyment ✔✔
Day activities ✘
Family camping ✘
Hard bushwalking ✘

23. Iron Range National Park

800 km N, 230 km N of Coen. North Coast, Tableland and Peninsula weather district. Main car access off Peninsula Developmental Road 94 km N of Coen; track impassable after heavy rains.

Animals found in New Guinea but recorded no farther south in Australia, such as the palm cockatoo, eclectus parrot and grey cuscus, have an important refuge in the undisturbed lowland rainforests of Iron Range. Semi-deciduous vines grow profusely throughout the forest and in thickets. Northern and western areas of this 35 000 ha wilderness reserve support eucalypts, turkey bush scrub on rocky slopes and stunted heath on the crests of the Janet and Tozer Ranges. Mangrove communities around the lower reaches of the Pascoe River include the unusual nypa or mangrove palm.

Little Roundback Hill, above the beaches of Weymouth Bay on the east of the park, was a depot for Edmund Kennedy's ill-fated expedition in 1848. Of eight men left here while Kennedy pushed on for Cape York, only two survived.
NOTE: Visitors must be fully equipped for outback survival.
BEST TIME: Winter.
TEL AND FAX: (07) 4060 7170.
ADDRESS: CMB 52, Portland Roads, Cairns Mail Centre 4871.

Scenic enjoyment ✔✔✔
Day activities ✘
Family camping ✔
Hard bushwalking ✘

24. Jardine River National Park

930 km N, 30 km S of Bamaga. North Coast, Tableland and Peninsula weather district. Vehicle access by 4WD only along rough track off Peninsula Developmental Road 120 km N of Coen; track impassable after heavy rains.

Eighteenth-century explorers named this vast wilderness in the Jardine River's catchment the 'wet desert'. The Jardine has Queensland's greatest year-round volume and water is abundant throughout the park. Vine scrubs, rainforest, sparse heathlands, swamps, overflow lagoons and grassless bogs full of poisonous plants made travel and even survival for early expeditions difficult or impossible.

The 235 000 ha national park remains virtually untouched and almost as forbidding to the best-equipped of modern 4WD safaris. A camping spot at the Jardine River crossing is one of the best known along the rough track to Cape York, but few travellers venture far from it.

Broad plateaux occupy much of the land around the head of the Jardine. Rainforest grows on the deepest soils, with eucalypt forest, heaths, scrub and bog vegetation elsewhere. Narrow depressions up to 30 m deep dissect the plateaux; many are swampy and give rise to fast-flowing streams. Swamp forest containing paperbarks, palms and vine forest plants has developed in some of the valleys. To the west scores of freshwater streams cross the low sandy coastline, flowing through vegetated dunes from a low escarpment at the northern end of the Great Dividing Range.
NOTE: Visitors must be fully equipped for outback survival.
BEST TIME: Winter.
TEL: (07) 4060 3241.
ADDRESS: PMB 76, Cairns Mail Centre 4871.

Scenic enjoyment ✔✔
Day activities ✘
Family camping ✘
Hard bushwalking ✘

25. Kurrimine National Park

125 km S, 10 km E of Silkwood. North Coast, Tableland and Peninsula weather district. Car access off Bruce Highway at Silkwood via Kurrimine Beach.

A low-lying strip of dense rainforest interspersed with scrub backs Cowley Beach just north of the resort township at Kurrimine Beach. Swampy wetlands with melaleucas, tea-trees, palms and grasses lie in a shallow depression behind the coastal forest fringe, hemmed in to the west by sandy soils supporting tea-tree, acacias and grass-trees. A short walking track loops through the southern part of the 910 ha park.
BEST TIME: Winter and spring.
TEL: (07) 4068 7183.
ADDRESS: As for Maria Creek.
Scenic enjoyment ✔✔
Day activities ✔
Family camping ✘
Hard bushwalking ✘

26. Lake Barrine (Crater Lakes National Park)

60 km SW, 35 km SW of Gordonvale. North Coast, Tableland and Peninsula weather district. Gillies Highway between Gordonvale and Atherton passes through the park.
DESCRIPTION: Page 131.
NOTE: Lake cruises daily all year. No camping allowed.
BEST TIME: Year-round.
TEL: (07) 4095 3768.
ADDRESS AND FAX: As for Lake Eacham.

Scenic enjoyment ✔✔✔
Day activities ✔✔✔
Family camping ✘
Hard bushwalking ✘

27. Lake Eacham (Crater Lakes National Park)

70 km SW, 45 km SW of Gordonvale. North Coast, Tableland and Peninsula weather district. Car access off Gillies Highway between Gordonvale and Yungaburra.
DESCRIPTION: Page 130. A further 5 ha of rainforest straddling Gillies Highway are preserved in the undeveloped **Yungaburra National Park,** 2 km SW of Yungaburra township.
NOTE: No camping allowed.
BEST TIME: Spring.
TEL: (07) 4095 3768.
FAX: (07) 4095 3403.
ADDRESS: PO Box 21, Yungaburra 4872.

Scenic enjoyment ✔✔✔
Day activities ✔✔
Family camping ✔
Hard bushwalking ✘

28. Lakefield National Park

390 km NNW, 146 km NW of Cooktown. North Coast, Tableland and Peninsula weather district. Car access off Peninsula Developmental Road from Laura; 4WD access from Cooktown via Battlecamp and from Coen via Musgrave and Saltwater Creek. Roads impassable after heavy rain.

A vast river system comprising main streams and tributaries of Bizant, Normanby, Hann, Morehead and North Kennedy Rivers drains this 537 000 ha park. During the wet season floodwaters break the banks of the rivers and join to form immense bodies of open water before emptying into Princess Charlotte Bay. The waters attract a huge population of birds, and even in the dry season swamps, creeks and lily-covered lagoons are home to countless brolgas, geese, ducks, cormorants, egrets and jabirus. Both fresh and saltwater crocodiles abound.

Many minor streams dry completely in winter, leaving bare

sandy beds. Beyond the watercourses grasslands and woodlands dominated by bloodwood, Darwin stringybark, Molloy red box and Moreton Bay ash spread out over the floodplains. Rainforest grows on rich soils along the river banks and mangroves line mudflats along the coast and estuary shores.

Lakefield is the most accessible of the parks of Cooktown. Rangers based at three former grazing station homesteads are well acquainted with its seasonal changes and visitors should take advantage of their advice on best spots for camping.
NOTE: Visitors must be fully equipped for outback survival.
BEST TIME: Winter.
TEL: (07) 4060 3271.
FAX: (07) 4060 3262.
ADDRESS: PMB 29, Cairns Mail Centre 4871.

Scenic enjoyment ✔✔
Day activities ✔
Family camping ✘
Walking, canoeing ✔✔

29. Lizard Island National Park

270 km N. North Coast, Tableland and Peninsula weather district. Flights Cairns–Lizard Island. Accessible by air or private boat.

Resort guests and campers stand in the footsteps of Lt James Cook at the lookout point on the highest peak of Lizard Island. Cook climbed to what is now known as Cook's Look in 1770 to search the Coral Sea for a safe passage through the outer ramparts of the Great Barrier Reef, just 20 km to the east.

Patches of coral reef virtually surround the island fringing a superb lagoon, popular for swimming and skin diving to view the underwater life of the reef.

Grassland covering most of the 1010 ha national park makes for easy walking to Cook's Look, between patches of open forest, heath and rainforest. Swamps form in shallow depressions fed by seasonal streams and mangroves line parts of the island's coast.

Seabird rookeries on coral cays and rocky outcrops south of Lizard Island are also protected as national parks. Mangroves dominate most of the six cays of the **Turtle Group** (91 ha), **Nymph Island** (65 ha) and **Two Islands** (15 ha). **Three Islands** (41 ha) supports a dense cover of grasses with low shrubs and casuarinas, and mangroves along the edge of a sheltered lagoon. Only the largest of the three rocky outcrops of **Rocky Islets** (32 ha) has substantial vegetation of woodland, scrub and grasses.
NOTE: One week camping limit.

BEST TIME: Winter.
TEL: (07) 4052 3096.
ADDRESS AND FAX: As for
Archer Bend.

Scenic enjoyment ✔✔✔
Day activities ✔✔
Family camping ✔
Hard bushwalking ✘

30. Maria Creek and Clump Mountain National Parks

Maria Creek 120 km S, 5 km SE of
Silkwood. North Coast, Tableland
and Peninsula weather district.
Access on foot from Murdering
Point road off Bruce Highway at
Silkwood. Clump Mountain 140
km S, 1 km S of Bingil Bay. Bingil
Bay–Mission Beach road skirts
park. Boat access from Kurrimine
Beach or Garners Beach.

Low palm swamps with scattered
tea-trees and patches of vine forest
on deeper soils spread over a 670
ha park hemmed in by the winding
arms of Maria and South Maria
Creeks. Grassland is patchily
distributed and eucalypts grow on
some low ridges. Mangroves line
the creek mouths as they join to
empty out to sea just south of
Kurrimine township.

On a clear day breaks in the tree
cover of Bicton Hill in **Clump
Mountain National Park** (300 ha)
give views over Maria Creek to
Mourilyan in the north and as far
as Hinchinbrook Island to the
south. A well-maintained walking
track from the Bingil Bay
beachfront road climbs gentle
slopes clothed in rainforest to the
hilltop lookout. Two smaller
patches of coastal rainforest
occupy parks of 26 ha and 4 ha
around Bingil Bay township.
NOTE: Picnic facilities at
Clump Mountain.
BEST TIME: Winter.
TEL: (07) 4068 7183.
ADDRESS: As for Hull River.

Scenic enjoyment ✔✔
Day activities ✔✔
Family camping ✘
Hard bushwalking ✘

31. Millstream Falls National Park

140 km SW, 7 km W of Ravenshoe.
North Coast, Tableland and
Peninsula weather district. Car
access off Kennedy Highway 5 km
W of Ravenshoe.
DESCRIPTION: Page 128.
NOTE: No camping allowed.
BEST TIME: Late autumn.
TEL: (07) 4097 6721.
ADDRESS AND FAX: As for
Lake Eacham.

Scenic enjoyment ✔✔✔
Day activities ✔✔
Family camping ✘
Hard bushwalking ✘

32. Mitchell and Alice Rivers National Park

670 km NW. North Coast,
Tableland and Peninsula weather
district. 4WD only via Kowanyama
off Burke Developmental Road at
Dunbar station.

Sparse woodlands and
grasslands occupy 37 000 ha of
alluvial plains in the fork of the
Mitchell and Alice Rivers. Galleries
of dense forest grow along the
rivers, which flow year-round.
NOTE: Permission for transit must
be pre-arranged with Kowanyama
Aboriginal Community. Permit
required for camping.
BEST TIME: Winter.
TEL: (07) 4094 7163.
FAX: (07) 4094 7213.
ADDRESS: Box 38, Chillagoe 4871.

Scenic enjoyment ✔
Day activities ✘
Family camping ✘
Hard bushwalking ✘

33. Mount Hypipamee National Park

105 km SW, 24 km S of Atherton.
North Coast, Tableland and
Peninsula weather district. Car
access off Kennedy Highway.
DESCRIPTION: Page 126.
BEST TIME: Winter.
TEL: (07) 4052 3096.
ADDRESS AND FAX: As for
Archer Bend.

Scenic enjoyment ✔✔
Day activities ✔✔
Family camping ✘
Hard bushwalking ✘

34. Mount Major (Tully Gorge National Park)

140 km SW, 7 km SE of
Ravenshoe. North Coast,
Tableland and Peninsula weather
district. Access on foot off
Ravenshoe–Vine Creek road.

The massive rhyolite bluff of Mt
Major (1174 m) towers above steep
slopes of vine jungle. Timbers
sought for commercial uses, such
as ash, silkwood, calophyllum,
yellow walnut and quandong, have
been protected from logging in the
rough, broken ground and are
preserved in the park, now part of
the 2210 ha **Tully Gorge NP**.
Walkers who reach the peak of the
mountain along Vine Creek pass
the 30 m drop of a forest-shrouded
waterfall. At the summit they gain
views over the Southern
Tableland, the slopes of Mt Fisher
to the north, and out to the coast.
BEST TIME: Spring.
TEL: (07) 4095 3768.
ADDRESS AND FAX: As for
Lake Eacham.
Scenic enjoyment ✔✔
Day activities ✘
Family camping ✘
Hard bushwalking ✔

35. Palmerston (Wooroonooran NP)

125 km S, 35 km W of Innisfail.
North Coast, Tableland and
Peninsula weather district.
Palmerston Highway crosses the
park.
DESCRIPTION: Page 135.
A smaller patch of rainforest at
Palmerston Rocks straddles the
Palmerston Highway 15 km W of
Innisfail. Similar forests are found
at **McNamee Creek,** an area of
1150 ha about 15 km from South
Johnstone now incorporated in the
park. Forestry tracks crossing the
park are rough, but generally
passable in dry conditions. The
course of the creek can be followed
on foot to small waterfalls, sandy
beaches and a number of spots
suitable for swimming.
BEST TIME: Winter.
TEL: (07) 4064 5115.
FAX: (07) 4064 5252.
ADDRESS: PO Box 800,
Innisfail 4860.

Scenic enjoyment ✔✔✔
Day activities ✔✔✔
Family camping ✔✔✔
Hard bushwalking ✘

36. Possession Island National Park

980 km N, 20 km N of Bamaga.
North Coast, Tableland and
Peninsula weather district.
Accessible by boat from Bamaga
and Thursday Island.

James Cook landed here in
August 1770 to complete his
Australian exploration and
formally claim the east coast down
to 38°S in the name of King
George III. The 500 ha island of
sandy beaches, mangrove swamps
and mudflats below a low, scrub-
covered ridge was declared a
national park for historical
reasons. An obelisk commemorates
Cook's visit.
BEST TIME: Winter.
TEL: (07) 4052 3096.
ADDRESS: As for Archer Bend.

Scenic enjoyment ✔
Day activities ✘
Family camping ✘
Hard bushwalking ✘

37. Rokeby (Mungkan Kandju National Park)

600 km N, 26 km N of Coen. North
Coast, Tableland and Peninsula
weather district. Access: Peninsula
Development Road through Coen
to the Rokeby access turnoff, then
west to Rokeby Ranger Station.

Rivers rising in the McIlwraith
Range take a long and winding
course across wide flood plains
before emptying into the Gulf of
Carpentaria 350 km to the west.
The Archer and Coen Rivers form
much of the boundary of this

section of the 547 000 ha park,
enclosing a variety of vegetation
types, a great number of bird
species and a big population of
freshwater crocodiles.
NOTE: Visitors must be fully
equipped for outback survival.
BEST TIME: Winter.
TEL: (07) 4060 3256.
ADDRESS: PMB 28, Cairns Mail
Centre 4871.

Scenic enjoyment ✔
Day activities ✘
Family camping ✘
Hard bushwalking ✘

38. Staaten River National Park

450 km W. North Coast, Tableland
and Peninsula weather district.
NO PUBLIC ACCESS.

Only scientists visit this 467 000
ha park. Termite mounds 2–3 m
high dot the vast open plains.
Broad-leafed tea-tree grows
extensively and galleries of
rainforest crowd close to the
permanent waters of the Staaten
River and its major tributaries:
Emu, Pandanus, Back and
Cockburn Creeks. Monsoonal rains
each summer force the rivers to
break their banks and spread over
sparsely wooded flood plains.
Inundation restricts the growth of
understorey vegetation. Instead,
grasses appear as the waters
subside.
NOTE: No camping permits are
issued for this park.
BEST TIME: Winter.
TEL: (07) 4052 3096.
FAX: (07) 4094 7213.
ADDRESS: Box 38, Chillagoe 4871.
Scenic enjoyment ✘
Day activities ✘
Family camping ✘
Hard bushwalking ✘

39. Starcke National Park

420 km N, 80 km N of Cooktown.
North Coast, Tableland and
Peninsula weather district. 4WD
only north from Cooktown via
Starcke station. Road impassable
after heavy rains.

Limestone-capped ridges and
plateaux around the headwaters of
the Starcke and Jack Rivers are as
rugged as any on Cape York
Peninsula. Weathering has
produced steep escarpments with
bare cliff faces rising from sea
level to over 400 m along the
eastern edge of this 8000 ha park.
Heaths and scrubs grow on the
exposed higher levels, with heavier
vegetation on deeply dissected
lower slopes and narrow valley
floors. Eucalypt communities and
well-developed rainforest are
widespread. Grassland are
patchily distributed on areas of
heavy basaltic soils.

To the south of Starcke station
homestead **Mount Webb National**

Park preserves a 414 ha remnant
of tall semi-deciduous vine forest
on a gently sloping hill rising to
400 m.
NOTE: Visitors must be fully
equipped for outback survival.
BEST TIME: Winter.
TEL: (07) 4052 3096.
ADDRESS AND FAX: As for
Archer Bend.

Scenic enjoyment ✔
Day activities ✘
Family camping ✘
Hard bushwalking ✔

40. Topaz Road National Park

95 km S, 24 km SE of Malanda.
North Coast, Tableland and
Peninsula weather district. Car
access via Lamins Hill off Lake
Eacham–Malanda road (part
unsealed).

Remnant rainforests of the
Atherton Tablelands lie
undisturbed along the narrow
gravel stretch of Topaz Road
among agricultural backblocks on
the slopes of Francis Range. The
park covers a trackless patch of
37 ha in rugged country at the
head of steep gullies with creeks
eventually feeding into upper
reaches of the Johnstone River.
NOTE: No camping allowed.
BEST TIME: Winter.
TEL: (07) 4095 3768.
ADDRESS AND FAX: As for
Lake Eacham.
Scenic enjoyment ✔
Day activities ✘
Family camping ✘
Hard bushwalking ✘

41. Tully Gorge National Park

160 km S, 24 km S of Ravenshoe.
North Coast, Tableland and
Peninsula weather district. Car
access from Ravenshoe.
DESCRIPTION: Page 129.
Waterfalls in national parks at
Elizabeth Grant Falls (480 ha) and
Cannabullen Falls (350 ha)
provide a more reliable spectacle
than the depleted flow through
Tully Gorge. But visitors need
good maps and detailed directions
from rangers to locate them in
steep gullies feeding into Tully
River from the east.
BEST TIME: Winter.
TEL: (07) 4095 3768.
ADDRESS AND FAX: As for
Lake Eacham.

Scenic enjoyment ✔✔
Day activities ✔✔
Family camping ✘
Hard bushwalking ✘

Birds, butterflies and wildlife in northern parks

In the north wildlife comes with all the exotic colour, abundance and size expected of the tropics. Everything is brighter and bigger. There are butterflies the size of birds – the Ulysses butterfly has a wingspan of about 100 millimetres. In the misty rainforests there are birds as bright as butterflies. There are, too, varieties of possum and glider not seen elsewhere, including oddities like the spotted cuscus, often mistaken for a monkey and creating alarming tales of illegal importation. Every park in the region has some part of this brilliant and fascinating selection of wildlife.

The green spotted triangle butterfly can be seen from Mackay to Cape York from January to May. It seems never to be still; even when feeding its wings are in constant motion

The Ulysses, or mountain blue, butterfly, one of the largest and most beautiful, is found only in rainforest where the corkwood tree grows

Buff-breasted paradise-kingfishers arrive from New Guinea early in November to establish breeding territory. By the end of April parents and young have gone

The purple-crowned superb fruit dove lives along the edge of northern rainforest

The mixture of yellow, grey, white and black in the green ringtail possum's coat creates the lime-green shade to the fur

The first indication a cassowary is near may be the rumbling sound the bird makes when it becomes aware of intruders

A dainty green tree frog displays its disced fingers and toes

Smallest member of the family, the golden bowerbird builds the biggest bower for its displays – two towers up to 3 metres high

155

Visitor activities in the national parks of Queensland

Aboriginal culture
Carnarvon; Chillagoe-Mungana Caves; Cooloola (Pipeclay); Lawn Hill; Snake Range.

Abseiling
Cape Hillsborough and Wedge Island; Carnarvon (permit required); Girraween; Moogerah Peaks; Mount Barney; Springbrook.

Aerial tours
Dryander.

Boat tours
Conway; Cooloola; Dryander; Dunk Island; Hinchinbrook Island; Hull River.

Bushwalking
Most national parks; consult individual entries for rating.

Burleigh Head is hemmed in by Gold Coast developments, but out on its headland it is possible to be away from it all

Reef walking in the clear waters off North West Island, moving slowly so as not to disturb the myriad marine life

Camping
Many national parks; consult entries.

Canoeing/boating
Barron Gorge; Bribie Island; Cape Palmerston; Cooloola; Cumberland Group; Dunk Island; Lakefield; Lakes Barrine and Eacham; Lawn Hill; Maria Creek; Sundown; Woody Island.

Car touring
Cape Hillsborough and Wedge Island; Chillagoe-Mungana Caves; Edmund Kennedy; Glass House Mountains; Magnetic Island.

Caving
Camooweal Caves; Chillagoe-Mungana Caves; Fitzroy Caves.

Cave tours
Chillagoe-Mungana Caves.

Fishing, freshwater
Cooloola; Lakefield; Maria Creek; Sundown; Woodgate.

Fishing, beach/ocean
Bowling Green Bay; Bribie Island; Burleigh Head; Cape Hillsborough and Wedge Island; Cape Palmerston; Capricorn Coast; Cooloola; Cumberland Group; Dryander; Dunk Island; Edmund Kennedy; Great Sandy; Keppel Bay; Magnetic Island; Maria Creek; Moreton Island; Noosa; Northumberland Islands; West Hill; Whitsunday Islands; Woody Island.

4-W driving
Cape Palmerston; Cape Tribulation; Cooloola; Dipperu; Great Sandy; Iron Range; Jardine River; Lakefield; Moreton Island; Rokeby; Sundown.

Geological studies
Black Mountain; Burleigh Head; Cape Hillsborough and Wedge Island; Carnarvon; Chillagoe-Mungana Caves; Cooloola; D'Aguilar Range; Girraween; Glass House Mountains; Isla Gorge; Lamington; Lawn Hill; Mount Fox; Pioneer Peaks; Robinson Gorge.

Historical studies
Carnarvon; Chillago-Mungana Caves; Cooloola; Endeavour River; Fort Lytton; Lawn Hill; Possession Island; Springbrook; St Helena Island.

Orienteering
Cape Palmerston; Carnarvon; Girraween; Isla Gorge; Robinson Gorge.

Power boating
Bribie Island; Cape Palmerston; Cooloola; Cumberland Group; Dunk Island; Keppel Bay; Lakefield; Lamington; Moreton Island; Northumberland Islands.

Rafting
Barron Gorge; Wooroonooran.

Rock climbing
Glass House Mountains; Moogerah Peaks; Mount Barney; Mount Fox.

Scuba diving/snorkelling
Cumberland Group; Dryander; Dunk Island; Frankland Islands; Gloucester and Middle Islands; Heron Island; Keppel Bay; Magnetic Island; Morton Island; Northumberland Islands; Orpheus Island; Whitsunday Islands; Woody Island.

Human visitors may camp on the shores of Lady Musgrave Island and dive off its reef from March to August. But for the rest of the year it is reserved as a nesting place for the brown gannets

An excellent way to explore the forested hills, heathlands and swamps in Cooloola National Park is to travel by canoe to the headwaters of the Noosa River

Young people strike off the track and use a creek as a path to make their own discoveries in Carnarvon National Park

A photographer attempts to capture the changing moods, shapes and colours of the Simpson Desert

Surfing
Bribie Island; Burleigh Head; Cooloola; Great Sandy; Moreton Island; Noosa.

Swimming
Blue Lake; Bowling Green Bay; Burleigh Head; Cape Hillsborough and Wedge Island; Cape Palmerston; Carnarvon; Conway; Cooloola; Crows Nest; Dryander; Dunk Island; Eungella; Girraween; Great Sandy; Jourama; Keppel Bay; Lakes Barrine and Eacham; Lamington; Lawn Hill; Magnetic Island; Moreton Island; Northumberland Islands; Orpheus Island; Springbrook; Tamborine; West Hill; Woody Island; Wooroonooran.

Walking along coastal tracks and beaches
Bowling Green Bay; Bribie Island; Burleigh Head; Cape Hillsborough and Wedge Island; Cape Palmerston; Capricorn Coast; Cooloola; Cumberland Group; Dryander; Dunk Island; Edmund Kennedy; Eungella; Hinchinbrook Island; Keppel Bay; Moreton Island; Noosa; West Hill.

Wildflowers
Alton; Burleigh Head; Carnarvon; Clump Mountain; Cooloola; Crows Nest; Edmund Kennedy; Girraween; Isla Gorge; Lakefield; Lamington; Maria Creek; Moogerah Peaks; Mount Barney; Reliance Creek; Robinson Gorge; Southwood; Woody Island.

Windsurfing
Burleigh Head; Cape Hillsborough and Wedge Island; Cooloola; Cumberland Group; Magnetic; Moreton Island; Whitsunday Islands.

Water skiing
Cooloola; Dunk Island.

Yachting
Cooloola; Cumberland Group; Dryander; Dunk Island; Hinchinbrook Island; Lizard Island; Magnetic Island; Moreton Island; Northumberland Islands; Whitsunday Islands.

CAMPING
Bush camping — away from it all, no facilities other than those you create.
Camping — a pit toilet and a tap but no other facilities.
Family camping — established camping ground with showers, toilets, barbecue areas and where you can probably take a caravan, but check beforehand.

INDEX

Protect our parks and wildlife

- Observe all fire bans.
- Use only fireplaces provided, or your own portable cooker.
- Don't take cats or dogs with you.
- Don't take firearms or other hunting weapons.
- Don't leave litter.
- Don't disturb or remove plants, rocks or animals.
- Obey 'No Entry' signs – they are for your safety, and also protect fragile areas.
- Keep your vehicle to formed roads and marked parking areas.

Addresses

Park Services

Environment Australia Biodiversity Group
GPO Box 636, Canberra ACT 2601 (02)6250 0200
Environment ACT
PO Box 144, Lyneham, ACT 2602, (02)6207 9777
New South Wales National Parks and Wildlife Service
PO Box 1967, Hurstville, NSW 2220, (02)9585 6444
Department of Environment
PO Box 155, Brisbane Albert Street, Qld, 4002,
(07)3227 7111
Queensland National Parks and Wildlife Service
PO Box 155, Brisbane Albert Street, Qld, 4002,
(07)3227 8186
Great Barrier Reef Marine Park Authority
PO Box 1379, Townsville, Qld, 4810, (07)4750 0700
South Australian National Parks and Wildlife Service
GPO Box 1047, Adelaide, SA, 5001, (08)8204 9000
Department of Environment and Land Management
Division of Conservation and Land Management
PO Box 44A, Hobart, Tasmania 7001. (03)6233 8011
Parks Victoria
Level 2, 35 Whitehorse Rd, Deepdene, Victoria 3103.
13 19 63
Department of Conservation and Land Management
Locked Bag 104, Bentley Delivery Centre, Western Australia
6983, (08)9334 0333

Park Associations

National Parks Association of the ACT
Maclaurin Crescent, Chifley ACT, 2606 (02)6282 5813
National Parks Association of NSW
PO Box A96, Sydney South, NSW 1235, (02)9223 4660
National Parks Association of Queensland
PO Box 1040, Milton, Queensland, 4064, (07)3367 0878
Nature Conservation Society of South Australia
120 Wakefield St, Adelaide, SA 5000 (08)8223 6301
Tasmanian Conservation Trust
102 Bathurst St, Hobart, Tasmania 7000, (03)6234 3552
Victorian National Parks Association
10 Parliament Place, East Melbourne, Victoria 3002,
(03)9650 8296
WA National Parks and Reserves Association
219 Railway Pde, Maylands, WA 6051, (08)9370 5901

Foundations for Conservation

Australian Conservation Foundation
Head Office : 340 Gore Street, Fitzroy, Victoria 3065.
(03)9416 1166
National Parks Foundation of South Australia
100 Currie St, Adelaide, SA 5000. (08)8231 0016
Foundation for National Parks and Wildlife
GPO Box 2666, Sydney, NSW 2001. (02)9337 3388

Australian Trust for Conservation Volunteers

Head Office : 15 Lydiard St, North Ballarat, Vic 3353.
(03)5333 1483
Vic : 534 City Rd, South Melbourne, Vic 3205.
(03)9686 5554
NSW : 2 Holt St, Stanmore, NSW 2048. (02)9654 1244
ACT : Old City Parks Depot, White Crescent, Campbell,
ACT. 2602 (02)6247 7770
Qld : Old Government House, George St, Brisbane, Qld
4000. (07)3210 0330
NT: 3 Harvey St, Darwin, NT 0800. (08)8981 9095
WA: 216 Queen Victoria St, North Fremantle, WA 6159.
(08)9336 6911
SA: State Tree Centre, Broadway Drive, Campbelltown, SA
5074. (08)8207 8747
Tas: Salamanca Arts Centre, Salamanca Place, Hobart, Tas
7000. (03)6224 4911

Wilderness Society

National Office : 130 Davey St, Hobart, Tas 7000.
(03)6234 9799

Bushwalking Federations

NSW : Bushwalking Federation of NSW, GPO Box 2090,
Sydney, NSW 1043, (02)9548 1228
Vic : VicWalk, 241 Swan St, Richmond, Vic 3121,
(03)9421 3100
Qld : Queensland Federation of Bushwalking Clubs,
GPO Box 1573, Brisbane, Qld 4001
WA: WA Federation of Bushwalking Clubs, PO Box 851,
Scarborough, WA 6922, (08)9362 1614
Tas : Federation of Tasmanian Bushwalking Clubs,
PO Box 1190, Launceston, Tasmania 7250.

Youth Hostels Association

NSW : 422 Kent St, Sydney, NSW 2000. (02)9261 1111
NT : 69 Mitchell St, Darwin, NT 0800. (08)8981 6344
Qld: 154 Roma St, Brisbane, Qld 4000. (07)3236 1680
SA: 38 Sturt St, Adelaide, SA 5000. (08)8231 5583
Tas: 28 Criterion St, Hobart, Tas 7000. (03)6234 9617
Vic: 205 King St, Melbourne, Vic 3000. (03)9670 7991
WA: 236 William St, Northbridge, WA 6003 (08)9227 5122

Acknowledgments

The publishers and editors are deeply indebted to administrators, interpretation officers and rangers of the various national parks services. Countless people spent long hours supplying or verifying information. Others assisted in planning the touring photographer's itineraries, or gave him considerable help in the field.

Thanks are also due to the staff of the National Herbarium, Royal Botanic Gardens, Sydney, for their assistance in plant identification, and to botanist A. R. Rodd.

Reference sources: The publishers acknowledge their indebtedness for information gained from the following books: *Atlas of Australian Resources* (Division of National Mapping); *Australia, a Timeless Grandeur*, Helen Grasswill (Landsdowne Press); *Australian Vegetation*, R. H. Groves, ed. (Cambridge University Press); *Australia's Endangered Species*, Derrick Ovington (Cassell); *Australia's 100 Years of National Parks* (NSW National Parks and Wildlife Service); *Complete Book of Australian Mammals*, Ronald Strahan, ed. (Angus and Robertson); *Discover Australia's National Parks*, Robert Raymond (Ure Smith); *Discover Australia's National Parks and Naturelands*, Michael and Irene Morcombe (Landsdowne Press); *Life on Earth*, David Attenborough (Reader's Digest-Collins-BBC); *National Parks of New South Wales*, Alan Fairley (Rigby); *National Parks of New South Wales* (Gregory's); *National Parks of Queensland*, Tony Groom (Cassell); *National Parks of Victoria*, Alan Fairley (Rigby); *National Parks of Victoria* (Gregory's); *National Parks of Western Australia*, C. F. H. Jenkins (National Parks Authority of WA); *Regional Landscapes of Australia*, Nancy and Andrew Learmonth (Angus and Robertson); *The Face of Australia*, C. F. Laseron, revised by J. N. Jennings (Angus and Robertson); *The Franklin Blockade*, Robin Tindale and Pam Waud, eds (Wilderness Society); *The Heritage of Australia* (Macmillan, Australian Heritage Commission); *The Value of National Parks* (Australian Conservation Foundation).

Photographs
Most photographs were taken by Robin Morrison, except for: (t = top, c = centre, b = bottom, l = left, r = right) Cover: The Photo Library. 11: t, Richard Woldendorp; b, Research School of Earth Sciences, ANU. 20: b, Photo Index. 28-9: Richard Woldendorp. 30: b, Dept of Conservation Forests & Lands, Vic. 31: l, cb, Sutherland Shire Library. 32: tl, bl & br, Dept of Conservation Forests & Lands, Vic. 33: tl, Ian Morris, Australian NPWS; br, Queensland NPWS. 34: Tasmanian NPWS. 35: cl, Tasmanian NPWS; tr, Bob Mossel; br, Jeffery Cutting. 36: tl, Queensland NPWS; b, Dept of Conservation Forests & Lands, Vic. 37: Conservation Commission of the NT. 38: tl & bl, Hans & Judy Beste; tr, Stephen Donellan; br, R. C. Lewis, CSIRO Division of Entomology. 39: tl, R. & A. Williams, National Photographic Index; tc & tr, Hans & Judy Beste; br, Ralph & Daphne Keller. 40: r, and 41:tl & br, Dept of Conservation Forests & Lands, Vic. 41: bc, Graham Robertson; tr, New South Wales NPWS. 42: t, C. Veitch. 71: R. V. Southcott. 90: Jean-Paul Ferrero/Auscape; b, Glen Threlfo/Auscape. 91: tl, G. B. Baker/ National Photographic Index; tr, bl, br, Hans & Judy Beste/ Auscape. 92: tl, F. Woerle/Auscape; tr, Jean-Paul Ferrero/ Auscape; bl, Graeme Chapman/Auscape. 92, and 93: tl, Jean-Paul Ferrero/Auscape. 93: tr, Graeme Chapman; br, F. Woerle/Auscape. 122: tl, The Photo Library; bl, Australian Institute of Marine Science. 123: The Photo Library. 154-5: all Hans & Judy Beste/Auscape. 156-7: Queensland NPWS.

Printed and bound by Dai Nippon Printing Co. Ltd, Hong Kong